INVASION OF PRIVACY

The *Cross Creek* Trial of
Marjorie Kinnan Rawlings

INVASION OF PRIVACY

The *Cross Creek* Trial of
Marjorie Kinnan Rawlings

Patricia Nassif Acton

Illustrated by J. T. Glisson

UNIVERSITY OF FLORIDA PRESS
Gainesville

†

University Presses of Florida is the central agency for scholarly publishing of the State of Florida's university system, producing books selected for publication by the faculty editorial committees of Florida's nine public universities: Florida A&M University Press (Tallahassee), Florida Atlantic University Press (Boca Raton), Florida International University Press (Miami), Florida State University Press (Tallahassee), University of Central Florida Press (Orlando), University of Florida Press (Gainesville), University of North Florida Press (Jacksonville), University of South Florida Press (Tampa), University of West Florida Press (Pensacola).

Orders for books published by all member presses should be addressed to University Presses of Florida, 15 NW 15th Street, Gainesville, FL 32603.

Contents

Note for the Future

Be kind to me,
Posterity.
Think tenderly
Of Marjorie.
On Zelma C.
Look stonily.
All curséd be
Who sueth me.

Poem written by Marjorie Kinnan
Rawlings during the *Cross Creek*
trial, May 1946.

The old Cross Creek bridge

Prologue

Meeting on the Bridge

For anyone who knows the northern Florida hamlet of Cross Creek well, it's not hard to tell the difference between a native and a newcomer. The native remembers the friendly wood and steel bridge that spanned the meandering link between Lakes Orange and Lochloosa known as Cross Creek. The newcomer knows only the modern concrete structure that now crosses the creek with impersonal efficiency.

The native also remembers the importance of the old bridge in keeping peace among the handful of families that called Cross Creek home. Feuding neighbors were urged by their fellow townsmen to "meet on the bridge." Interested spectators gathered on both banks of the creek to watch the combatants settle their disputes with fists or a handshake. Then the feud was forgotten and peace returned to Cross Creek.

So the old bridge was a symbol of unity for this tiny community of Florida crackers.* The community's problems were solved by its own people. Outside interference was neither wanted nor needed. Marjorie Kinnan Rawlings said it best in her masterwork *Cross Creek:* "We know that in our relations with one another, the disagreements are unimportant and the union vital."

Marjorie had come to Cross Creek in 1928. She was tired of life in large northern cities and discouraged by her prospects as a writer. The isolation and lush beauty of the half-wild Florida countryside stirred her imagination. She was moved by the quiet dignity and friendliness of her modest neighbors. Here, she decided, she

*A nickname for natives of Florida and Georgia, often used by the natives themselves with pride.

would write something good or admit finally that she was no writer at all.

Marjorie abandoned her former literary efforts and began to write stories inspired by her cracker neighbors. The books emerged in quick succession, and Marjorie became world-famous. In 1939 she won a Pulitzer Prize for *The Yearling*, a novel about a boy's coming of age in the lonely Florida scrub country. In 1942 she published the highly acclaimed *Cross Creek*, an introspective, often hilarious sketchbook of life in her adopted community. Marjorie described the book as "a love story."

One of the characters in *Cross Creek* was Zelma Cason, a feisty and controversial inhabitant of nearby Island Grove. Marjorie met Zelma the first day she arrived in Florida, and they became close friends. Marjorie once accompanied Zelma on horseback to take the local census. She wrote about their adventures in the chapter "The Census," which began with a colorful description of Zelma:

> Zelma is an ageless spinster resembling an angry and efficient canary. She manages her orange grove and as much of the village and county as needs management or will submit to it. I cannot decide whether she should have been a man or a mother. She combines the more violent characteristics of both and those who ask for or accept her manifold ministrations think nothing of being cursed loudly at the very instant of being tenderly fed, clothed, nursed or guided through their troubles.

Zelma Cason was furious when she read this. She complained to friends that she had never consented to be in the book, and she was humiliated by Marjorie's description. When Marjorie visited her with an autographed copy of *Cross Creek*, Zelma burst into an angry tirade. "You have made a hussy out of me," she fumed.

Marjorie apologized, and the two women talked. Marjorie left, satisfied that their friendship was restored.

She was wrong. Within a few months of this meeting, Zelma Cason filed a lawsuit against the celebrated author for invasion of her "right of privacy." The suit was a shock in more ways than one. Marjorie couldn't believe that her old friend had turned against her. And she was even more surprised at the nature of the lawsuit. Never before had a disgruntled literary subject claimed invasion of a "right of privacy" in a suit against the author of an autobiographical work. The state of Florida hadn't even recognized the existence of such a right. But Zelma was determined to defend her privacy, even if it meant a long legal battle.

Zelma wasn't alone in her fight. She had found a remarkable attorney—Kate Walton of Palatka. "Miss Kate," as she was called, was one of the first women to be admitted to the Florida bar. At a time when women could not serve on Florida juries, or sue without joining their husbands, "Miss Kate" guided the untested privacy claim through five-and-a-half years of tortuous legal proceedings. The litigation culminated in a much publicized trial before a Gainesville jury, featuring a cast of characters from country lawyer Sigsbee Scruggs to a parade of cracker witnesses who testified to Zelma's famous profanity. The case was appealed twice to the Florida Supreme Court. The outcome was surprising and disappointing for everyone.

But the story of the *Cross Creek* trial is more than just the story of a bitterly fought legal battle. In bringing the lawsuit, an offense greater than that charged to Marjorie was inflicted on the peace of Cross Creek. For once, the injured parties failed to meet on the bridge. Zelma and Marjorie could not—or would not—settle their dispute in the bosom of the community. Friendly dialogue was exchanged for the formalism of a courtroom. The smooth efficiency of the legal system, like the concrete bridge that would soon span Cross Creek, replaced the familiar means of solving problems among neighbors. And the lives of those touched by this unique and dramatic controversy would never be altogether the same.

Chapter One

A Love Story

If asked, Marjorie Kinnan Rawlings would surely have described herself as a native of Cross Creek. Who but a native could write so fondly and honestly of a place and its people? Her coming to the Creek had been less an arrival than a homecoming. She fought the ties that bound her to the North. "I have always considered myself a Southerner," she declared. "Anyone calls me a Yankee at his peril."

Marjorie Kinnan was born on August 8, 1896, in Washington, D.C., the daughter of an attorney in the U.S. Patent Office. She was raised in the suburb of Brookland, but many happy summer weeks were spent exploring the woods and fields of her father's Maryland farm. Her love of nature was fueled by these rural adventures, and by visits to her maternal grandfather's farm in Michigan. Marjorie's penchant for writing was soon apparent, and she won a $2.00 prize for a story published in the *Washington Post*. She was eleven years old.

When Marjorie was seventeen, her beloved father died. Marjorie finished high school in Washington and then moved with her mother and younger brother to Madison, Wisconsin. There she attended the University of Wisconsin, where she enthusiastically threw herself into extracurricular activities. Her associations included the Dixie Club, Phi Beta Kappa, and the staff of the University of Wisconsin *Lit*, the campus literary magazine. At the *Lit* she met Charles Rawlings, like Marjorie an aspiring writer.

Marjorie graduated in 1918 with a degree in English.

By then she and Charles were engaged, and Charles was scheduled to begin military training on Long Island. Marjorie moved to New York City to be closer to Charles and to launch a career in writing. She found work as an editor for the National Board of the YWCA, but she was disappointed in efforts to publish her portfolio of poems and stories.

Marjorie and Charles were married in 1919, and spurning Marjorie's dream of a grand adventure in Europe, they lived in New York City, Louisville, Kentucky, and finally in Charles's hometown of Rochester, New York. Charles worked briefly as a publicity agent for an export firm and later as a traveling salesman for his father's shoe company. Marjorie continued to write poetry and short fiction, but the popular magazines rejected her work. Both she and Charles had more success with journalism, working on the staffs of Louisville and Rochester newspapers. Charles was a reporter specializing in boating events; Marjorie was a feature writer and a syndicated columnist. From 1926 to 1928 the undomesticated Marjorie wrote a daily feature called "Songs of the Housewife," eventually syndicated in about fifty newspapers.

In March of 1928 Marjorie and Charles sailed from New York to enjoy a brief vacation in Florida with Charles's brothers. Wray and James Rawlings lived in the tiny town of Island Grove, where they were friendly with the Cason family. When Marjorie and Charles pulled into the Clyde Steamship Line dock at Jacksonville, they were met by none other than Zelma Cason, who escorted them to points in the city. They then traveled inland to join the Rawlings brothers, and for the next two weeks they fished, boated, and tramped through the lush beauty of northern Florida.

Marjorie was captivated by the exotic countryside and its isolated but friendly inhabitants. She decided that this was where she wanted to live and write. Here she might forget the strains of career, marriage, and city life and begin anew. Years later, during her testimony at the *Cross Creek* trial, she was questioned about her decision to live in Florida:

Q: What was your reaction to Florida?
A: It seemed to me that I had arrived home at last. I had been very unhappy living in the North and in cities.
Q: Did you make any determination on that trip with reference to your future home?
A: Yes. My husband asked, on the last day of our visit in Island Grove, "How would you like to be the wife of an orange grower?" I said, "I was about to ask you how you would like to be the husband of one."

The young couple returned to New York, after instructing the Rawlings brothers to locate a Florida grove where they could support themselves and their writing. In July, brother Wray wrote to recommend purchase of "the Armstrong place," a 74-acre citrus and pecan grove on the shore of Orange Lake in nearby Cross Creek. With over 2,000 trees, farmhouse, tenant house, chickens, and the like, the place seemed ideal. Sight unseen, Marjorie and Charles agreed to the purchase. Marjorie used an inheritance derived from the sale of her father's farm as a down payment. The couple sold their home in Rochester and moved to Florida in November of 1928. They were joined at the Creek by the two Rawlings brothers.

Marjorie never looked back. She was drawn to her new home with a passion she captured in the opening pages of *Cross Creek*:

When I came to the Creek, and knew the old grove and farmhouse at once as home, there was some terror, such as one feels in the first recognition of a human love, for the joining of person to place, as of person to person, is a commitment to shared sorrow, even as to shared joy.

For Marjorie, the union of person to place was complete. With success and passing years she would acquire other houses, but her heart remained in the old farmhouse at Cross Creek. Almost twenty years later she confided at the trial: "I never had a home elsewhere than Cross Creek."

Fueled with enthusiasm, Marjorie surmounted hardships that would try the mettle of the most seasoned farmer. Drought, freezes, and fruit flies were the hard reality beneath the idyllic vision of life at Cross Creek. Marjorie, Charles, and the two brothers tended the grove, planted crops, cared for the animals, and repaired the old homestead and outbuildings. The couple's modest capital was depleted, and there were no immediate returns from their writings. Still, Marjorie was not discouraged. In March of 1930 she wrote to the editor of *Scribner's Magazine*, which had just accepted her first story for publication: "My past years have become somehow unimportant. They are a shadow, against the satisfying substance that is our life in the heart of the Florida hammock.... We do not expect ever to regret the move."

But Marjorie spoke only for herself, not for her fellow adventurers. After a year, James Rawlings left to take a job in the North. Brother Wray left soon after. Charles Rawlings, whose articles on yachting and other nautical themes were now a modest success, grew increasingly restive under the discipline and disappointments of Cross Creek life. Charles wanted to sell the grove; Marjorie did not. Their problem-ridden marriage was strained beyond its limits. Charles left Cross Creek, and in November of 1933 the couple was divorced. Marjorie, with characteristic courage and determination, decided to stay and "fight it out."

Marjorie's house at Cross Creek

This personal crisis came at a time when Marjorie's literary career was at last taking off. Her enchantment with Cross Creek unleashed a torrent of creative energies. She filled notebooks with stories about life at the Creek, and she decided to abandon all attempts to write "from a popular angle." Instead, she would write about her cracker neighbors and the joys and hardships of "this wild, beautiful country." If she didn't succeed, Marjorie resolved that she would give up writing.

She didn't have to give up. Under the guiding influence of editor Maxwell E. Perkins of Charles Scribner's Sons, whose other protegés included F. Scott Fitzgerald, Ernest Hemingway, and Thomas Wolfe, Marjorie's pen captured the charm and richness of her surroundings. In early 1931 two of her stories appeared in the prestigious *Scribner's Magazine*. "Cracker Chidlings" was a collection of sketches and local color; "Jacob's Ladder" was the story of a young cracker couple's nomadic life in northern Florida. Other short stories followed.

Marjorie's first novel, *South Moon Under*, was published in 1933. The novel was set in the Big Scrub, a wilderness plateau twenty-odd miles southeast of Cross Creek bounded by the Oklawaha and St. Johns Rivers. To prepare for the book, Marjorie had spent over two months in the Big Scrub with a cracker family, hunting and fishing illegally, moonshining, and tasting the rugged, spare life of the few human inhabitants. *South Moon Under* was praised by the critics and offered as a selection by the Book-of-the-Month Club.

This stunning literary debut was followed in 1935 by the less successful *Golden Apples*, a novel about an Englishman exiled to the lush wilds of northern Florida and his relationship to young cracker squatters. Then in 1938 came *The Yearling*, a novel about a twelve-year-old boy whose lonely existence in the Big Scrub is eased by the friendship of a pet fawn. The book was hailed as a literary masterpiece and was translated into thirteen languages. Film rights were promptly sold to MGM, and Marjorie was awarded the Pulitzer Prize for fiction. A collection of short stories entitled *When the Whippoorwill* was published in 1940.

All of Marjorie's fictional works sprang from the notes and stories she collected during her first years at Cross Creek. But she had other, more intimate plans for this material. She believed that her greatest work would be a personal account of the place that had so inspired her. She would later testify at the *Cross Creek* trial: "I had always known ever since I had been in Florida that some day I would write about my own life in that immediate small community." The result was the enormously successful *Cross Creek*, published in 1942.

As early as 1935 Marjorie had written to Max Perkins that she wanted to publish a book about her life at Cross Creek, "catching, I hope, the quality that has made me cling so desperately and against great odds to this place." Two years later she brought up the subject again, informing him that the book would be called *Cross Creek: A Chronicle*. In 1938, when Marjorie was scheduled to undergo a life-threatening operation, she wrote Perkins that she had no fear of death, but *Cross Creek: A Chronicle* would be "the only thing about which I should feel that something was undone." Perkins encouraged Marjorie in the venture. "It would make a beautiful book," he wrote.

Marjorie worked steadily on *Cross Creek* through most of 1940 and 1941. For Marjorie writing was "a peculiar anguish," but this book was a labor of love. She later explained her feelings at the trial: "To me 'Cross Creek' is a love story. It is a story of my love for the land, and for that particular portion of the land where I have felt that I belonged, which is Cross Creek."

Cross Creek was an immediate hit. The first of many trade editions was published in February of 1942. It was chosen as a Book-of-the-Month Club selection and was also published in a special armed forces edition, read by thousands of servicemen during World War II. Four years later the acclaim of critics and the glow of public approval would become an integral part of Marjorie's defense at the trial.

Although *Cross Creek* sprang from the same soil as Marjorie's other writings, it was a work that defied conventional literary description. Uproarious as well as introspective, the book has no specific chronology or plot structure. Instead, it is a loosely woven fabric of sketches, impressions, and narrative description, the warp and woof of life at Cross Creek. At the trial Marjorie explained that her purpose in writing *Cross Creek* was to "interpret ... this lovely country and these people as they appealed to me." Consequently, the book revealed more of Marjorie's heart and soul than her personal history.

The precise character of *Cross Creek* became an issue in the lawsuit, with Zelma Cason claiming that the book "was advertised for sale and sold as a true account of the life and sojourn of the said Marjorie Kinnan Rawlings in the Florida backwoods, but was, as a matter of fact, in large part devoted to gossipy and scandalous tales and accounts ... of the private lives of her friends." Marjorie's lawyers responded that the book was "purely an autobiography," but Marjorie undoubtedly came closer to the truth when she testified that *Cross Creek* was a "limited selective autobiography." In fact, she had confided to Perkins shortly before the book's publication: "I did not want anything like an autobiography of these past thirteen years. I wanted the thing objective, the only subjectivity consisting of my personal reaction to the Creek, its natural aspects and its people."

This element of "subjectivity" made Marjorie vulnerable at the trial to the charge that she fictionalized certain events, distorting a purportedly factual picture of her neighbors. All this was irrelevant to Zelma's claim of invasion of privacy, as the Florida Supreme Court would eventually rule, but it was the stuff of which good cross-examination was made. Zelma's lawyer questioned Marjorie vigorously about a passage in *Cross Creek* where she wrote: "I have used a factual background for most of my tales, and of actual people a blend of the true and the imagined. I myself cannot quite tell where the one ends and the other begins." How then could Marjorie discern fact from fiction in *Cross Creek*, particularly the passages concerning Zelma Cason? Marjorie admitted that she had "rearranged" several stories, but she insisted that "there is as little fiction in it as you could possibly have in a book of that type." As to the chapter on Zelma, "nothing is imagined."

This was not the first time Marjorie was forced to defend the accuracy of her writings. She knew well the risks of writing about real people and places. Injured feelings, resentment, and the threat of lawsuits were genuine concerns for any author. Marjorie was no exception, as she learned from her earliest days as a published writer. Her first brush with controversy occurred in 1931, with the publication of "Cracker Chidlings." An editorial in the *Ocala Evening Star* accused Marjorie of distortion and ignorance of the Florida back country. Marjorie was hospitalized for an appendectomy when the editorial was published, and it was kept from her until the day she was released from the hospital. She promptly defended her article in an indignant letter to the editor:

My artistry I cannot myself becomingly defend. Of my accuracy I am so positive that I feel, in good time, as your knowledge increases, you will offer me the courtesy of an apology. My dear sir, my sketches are so true, that I have softened, not colored them, for fear that if they came to the chance attention of the subjects—all within a forty-mile radius of my home—offense would be taken at my frankness, where none was intended.

"Jacob's Ladder," published soon after, also received some local criticism. Max Perkins comforted the budding author following these public attacks on her writings: "Anything written about a given region, even in a tone of highest compliment, is always objected to. We might have warned you." Marjorie was also warmly consoled by Zelma Cason, whom Marjorie described as "my staunch supporter."

Marjorie had to deal with another kind of fall-out from the publication of "Cracker Chidlings." One of the "Chidlings" sketches, entitled "The Preacher Has His Fun," was introduced with this sentence: "Gus Teeter and Harry Barnes and a handful more have given their town a bad name." Harry Barnes was the actual name of a local youth. Marjorie had not taken the precaution of fictionalizing his name, as she had with the other characters. She was unaware that Barnes had lingering disabilities suffered in World War I and had died tragically before "Chidlings" was published. Not surprisingly, Barnes's mother was irate.

Zelma Cason decided to act the role of peacemaker. She may have felt responsible for Marjorie's troubles, since it was she who had told Marjorie the story on which the sketch was based. Or she may have felt the problem warranted intervention of a home-grown type, since Marjorie was still a "Yankee" in the eyes of the locals. In any event, it was clear something had to be done. Zelma testified at the *Cross Creek* trial that Barnes's mother was "very much upset" and "rode backwards and forwards in front of [Marjorie's] house." And Marjorie was physically incapacitated, still recuperating from her appendectomy. So Zelma Cason was the logical person to take matters in hand.

Zelma drove Marjorie to the home of Barnes's mother.

The mother refused to come to the car, but Zelma persuaded the woman's sister to hear their apology. Marjorie later recounted that Zelma "handled it very beautifully and very tactfully," informing the sister "that no offense was meant and none should be taken, that I was a writer and just used material as it came up and it had no thought of offending."

Zelma's intervention was successful, and the threatening behavior stopped. Two years later Marjorie and Barnes's mother met at a barbecue. Marjorie approached the woman and told her she was "very unhappy to hurt her." The woman replied: "I understand. I wish you would have known Harry, you would have liked him." She added, with obvious sincerity, "You're a good woman."

Marjorie had other reasons for concern over the authentic nature of her writings. Following publication of *South Moon Under*, she worried that the close identity of fictional characters and her real-life friends might attract the unwanted attention of the law. To gather material for the novel, Marjorie had lived for several weeks with a cracker family in the scrub. The son, Leonard Fiddia, eked out a precarious living from the exhausted land by moonshining and illegal hunting.

Marjorie had gone over the manuscript of *South Moon Under* with Leonard, so she did not fear his reaction. But she knew that parts of the novel were "photographic," and she was concerned that promotional publicity might alert the authorities to Leonard's moonshining. So she wrote Perkins, urging him to be careful:

It's not a question, as it was in the "Cracker Chidlings" of hurting people's feelings by writing them up, and of bothering the Chamber of Commerce type of person. . . . It would be a matter of actually getting a definite family in trouble with the law by identifying them too publicly with my book-characters. I have been nervous about that part of it from the beginning.

For the most part, Marjorie marveled at the generosity of her friends in sharing their knowledge and experiences with her. Of one friend, reptile expert Ross Allen, she wrote: "[H]e could have written and sold the story of our snake-hunt himself and received good money for it, whereas it is I who has made the fabulous profits. . . . Yet he is pleased to be a part of the larger pattern." But she occasionally encountered resentment. While writing *The Yearling* she went bear-hunting and listened to the yarns of a "marvelous old pioneer" in the scrub, Barney Dillard. Marjorie reported that his children feared she was appropriating the old man's life story. She soon won them over, however, with her sincerity and good humor.

Marjorie also encountered the plagiarism claims that often follow artistic success. Several years after publication of *The Yearling* she was contacted by the lawyer of a California woman who accused Marjorie of infringing the story of the woman's pet deer. Marjorie's lawyer informed the complainant that any similarity between the two deer was coincidental, "as Mrs. Rawlings never heard of your client, her deer, or the article to which you refer." Marjorie was not troubled with the complaint again.

Such problems took on special importance as Marjorie prepared to publish *Cross Creek*. By Marjorie's count, the book contained 121 identified characters, and their stories were both hilarious and poignant. Marjorie sought the advice of Max Perkins:

Now I have used true names in practically every instance. I have tried not to put things so that anyone's feelings would be hurt. These people are my friends and neighbors, and I would not be unkind for anything, and though they are simple folk, there is the possible libel danger to think of. What do you think of this aspect of the material?

Perkins replied with a suggestion that Marjorie "amend" the description of an unnamed country lawyer in the chapter entitled, "Black Shadows." (The unnamed lawyer was none other than Sigsbee Scruggs, who later co-counseled Marjorie's defense at the *Cross Creek* trial.) But Perkins seemed otherwise unconcerned about the risk of libel. "I doubt if there is any real danger," he wrote, "because of the character of the people ... but you are the one who must be the judge." Marjorie did take a few extra precautions. Perhaps recalling her problems with "Cracker Chidlings," she fictionalized two or three persons' names to avoid their unnecessary embarrassment. And she decided to pay personal visits to two of her neighbors to ask how they would feel about publication of *Cross Creek*. If they had no objections, then surely her instincts about the good will of everyone else in the book would be confirmed.

The first visit was to Tom Glisson, Marjorie's nearest neighbor at Cross Creek. After the usual niceties, Glisson declared, "I know you must have something in mind, or you wouldn't be walking up here in this hot sun." Marjorie explained that she was writing a book about Cross Creek, using real names and stories. "I have had to color the book," she admitted, explaining that she had eliminated some incidents and changed the chronology of others. "I wondered what you would think about that, and how other people would feel about it?" Glisson could speak only for himself, but his words were encouraging. "Marge," he said, "People who know me, know me. People who don't know me, I don't give a damn. If you can sell that kind of stuff, you do it."

Marjorie was considerably more nervous about the second visit. After Perkins's letter urging her to "be the judge" of her neighbors' reactions, she pored over her manuscript again. She concluded that if anyone would be offended, it would be "Mr. Martin" in the chapter "A Pig Is Paid For." In that chapter she recounted the tale of Mr. Martin's marauding pigs, who repeatedly destroyed Marjorie's fluffy-ruffle petunias. When the offense became too much for her to bear, she picked up her gun and shot the porcine ringleader. She then had a tense but humorous encounter with Mr. Martin, during which Marjorie agreed to make retribution, but without contrition: "Oh, Mr. Martin," she declared, "I did so enjoy shooting that pig."

Now Marjorie decided to face Mr. Martin again, this time with the page proofs of *Cross Creek* in hand. She marched to the Martin house and confronted the issue head-on. "Mr. Martin," she said, "I thought the argument we had over the pig and the way it all came out made an awfully good story.... I would like to read you what I had written about it." Marjorie nervously read the story aloud as Mr. and Mrs. Martin sat by their fireplace. Neither one cracked a smile. At the end of the reading Mr. Martin rose, stretched, and—to Marjorie's supreme relief—chuckled. "That's O.K.," he announced.

Marjorie left, satisfied that she had cleared the last hurdle to the book's acceptance. So certain was she of Martin's approval that she later thought about calling him as a defense witness. "Mr. Martin is proud to be in the book," she wrote to her attorney.

But Marjorie knew from experience that there were bound to be some feathers to unruffle. It was one thing to imagine one's life in a book; it was another to see it in black and white. She remained confident that "[m]ost of the friends written about in 'Cross Creek' can be counted on without insulting them by asking them how they feel ... about it." Still, she couldn't resist the urge to talk with some of them after *Cross Creek* was published to glean the local reaction.

When she ran into Old Joe MacKay in a Gainesville

Marjorie reads "A Pig Is Paid For"
to Mr. and Mrs. Martin

hardware store, Marjorie asked him: "You didn't mind my mentioning you in my book, 'Cross Creek', did you?" MacKay smiled and said, "Why, no, I was glad." But Marjorie was "floored" to learn that MacKay hadn't read the book, an omission she quickly remedied by giving him an autographed copy. She also called on the Townsend family, featured in "The Pound Party" chapter. Marjorie inquired of Mrs. Townsend: "I hope you took it as a compliment when I wrote about you in 'Cross Creek'?" Mrs. Townsend responded sweetly: "Yes, indeed, we enjoyed it. You wrote so nice about our little party."

At least publicly, Marjorie's neighbors kept their peace and remained silent about the book's impact. If people were hurt or troubled by the humorous liberties taken with their characters, they nurtured their wounds in private. Pride may have kept them from speaking out. Admiration for the world-famous author may also have contributed to their silence. Many of them were just plain fond of Marjorie, like Annie Slater, immortalized in the chapter "The Widow Slater." Marjorie realized she had "made a bit of mild fun" of her friend, yet Mrs. Slater wrote generously to Marjorie before the trial: "[I]t was fun to read Cross Creek—everything seemed so natrel [sic]—so like real life—I don't see how anyone could find fault with what is said in it." Others were simply resigned to the facts, like friend Dessie Smith, whose exploits were chronicled in "Hyacinth Drift." "Hell," said Dessie. "The truth is the truth!"

But there were undeniable rumblings of dissatisfaction over the sea of calm. A few months after *Cross Creek* was published Marjorie received an irate letter from a Tennessee relative of George Fairbanks, of whom Marjorie had written:

The great Fairbanks family itself has been sifted by time and circumstance until only George is left to carry the name. He carries it in an amazing body, bony and gangling, with no chin at all, a black mustache, the whole dressed loosely in nondescript garments topped by an immense black Stetson hat. The effect is a parody of the villain in an old-fashioned melodrama. He is gentleness itself, except when corn liquor inflames him and the Fairbanks blood runs hot, and stuttering, he tells any man on earth what he thinks of him.

Fairbanks's relative was incensed by Marjorie's description. "Is it kind to make copy out of anyone's limitations or misfortunes?" she wrote. "I am surprised that any author today would publish a book giving true names of persons who are still alive." Marjorie waited a few weeks before responding:

> I think you completely missed the point I made about George Fairbanks. That point was that for all his unfortunate circumstances, he still maintained his integrity and pride. George himself did not find my story about him at all offensive, and neither did any of the other people at the Creek.

Marjorie may have taken some comfort from the fact that it was Fairbanks's relative, and not Fairbanks himself, who had taken offense. But the letter was an ominous signal that all was not well. Marjorie was concerned when the daughter of Old Boss Brice—a character mentioned in *Cross Creek*—was "cool" to her during a neighborly visit. She felt relieved when Old Boss himself put his arm around her, a gesture she took as "tacit support."

She was also worried by rumors that another *Cross Creek* subject, neighbor Tom Morrison, was contemplating a lawsuit. Marjorie summoned up her courage and went to visit him. "You didn't mind my mentioning you, did you?" she asked. "Why, no," Morrison replied. Marjorie offered him a copy of *Cross Creek*, but Morrison declined, explaining that he had already read it. Instead, he asked for a copy of Marjorie's newly published cookbook, *Cross Creek Cookery*. In relief she "rushed him my own Creek copy, again, tenderly inscribed, 'To my good friend of many years' standing.'"

Unknown to Marjorie at the time, someone was agitating the quiet waters of Cross Creek. That someone was Zelma Cason. After *Cross Creek* was published Zelma made an angry visit to Tom Glisson, demanding to know what he "aimed to do." Glisson told Zelma he didn't aim to do anything: "If Marge can come to Cross Creek and make a living writing about the people here, joy go with her." He added: "Friendship is worth more to me than any amount of money." Zelma wasn't satisfied with Glisson's answer. "I'm just not going to take it," she warned.

If people at the Creek shared Zelma's sentiments, she was unable to rouse them to action. A friend wrote to Marjorie that he had learned of others besides Zelma who resented *Cross Creek*, but "[n]one of them knew how or had the courage to object to it." Marjorie probably doubted this appraisal of her neighbors' feelings. If they were indeed offended, it wasn't fear that kept them quiet. It was friendship and loyalty. After the lawsuit was filed and the floodtide of neighborly support rolled in, Marjorie wrote to her attorney with heartfelt gratitude: "Phil, these people are so damn *sweet.*"

"Sweet" was not a word most folks would choose to describe Zelma Cason. Even so, Zelma was not someone who Marjorie suspected would turn against her. "I thought Zelma and I were good friends," she remarked ingenuously, "and never dreamed she would take offense." After all, Marjorie had known Zelma since her first day in Florida. And though her friendship with

Zelma had cooled, Marjorie continued to visit Zelma's mother (whom she affectionately called "Mother Cason") in Island Grove, and Zelma's brother, T. Z., was her personal physician. There was no risk of estranging the Cason family. Or so Marjorie thought.

Marjorie had very nearly excluded Zelma altogether in her writing of *Cross Creek*. She finally included the chapter "The Census" despite her concern that it lacked interest, in order to acquaint readers with the local scene. The chapter described Marjorie's travels on horseback with Zelma to take the census of Alachua County. Marjorie explained at the trial that Zelma had asked her along "for the fun and interest," and also because "Zelma knew that my mind and heart were constantly open to people and places that would eventually become part of a story or another book."

The first draft of "The Census" did not include the fateful description of Zelma. When the draft was returned to Marjorie there was a handwritten note from Max Perkins: "'My friend Zelma' is a wonderful character. You must have a description of her." Marjorie obediently complied. Under her imaginative pen, "my friend Zelma" was transformed from a faceless appellation to a lively personality. Readers might forget the rest of the chapter, but few could forget that Zelma was "an ageless spinster resembling an angry and efficient canary." It was a description that Zelma Cason could not forget—or forgive.

Marjorie herself believed that the description was a "practically accurate" picture of Zelma. This assessment was enthusiastically seconded by Tom Glisson's son, J. T., who later commented: "It's probably the most perfect description that's ever been written about anyone. It was deadly accurate." Even Zelma's niece, in an interview forty years after the trial, was exuberant in her praise of Marjorie's accuracy: "There isn't anybody in

Island Grove who knew [Zelma] that wouldn't agree. What Marge Rawlings said about her is the truth. That's the way she was!"

In fact, Marjorie was so sure of Zelma's approval that she hastened to present her with an autographed copy of *Cross Creek* soon after its publication. The meeting took place in April 1942 in the St. Augustine house where Zelma was boarding. Marjorie greeted Zelma in the entryway with a copy of *Cross Creek*, inscribed: "For my good friend Zelma Cason, with affection, Marjorie Kinnan Rawlings." Zelma icily informed Marjorie that she could have saved herself a trip because she, Zelma, wanted no part of it. At the trial, Zelma gave this account of what she said:

> I told her she had humiliated me; and as far as my own true friends are concerned they will stick by me like Panther's Fertilizer, "time-tried and tested," but I may not have many of this kind. I told her she had tried to hurt me, she did it on purpose.

Marjorie was "surprised and disturbed." Putting aside her plans to hurry off, she sat down and began to cry. "Zelma," she said, "I don't understand; everyone that has spoken of it to me thinks it is a cute and attractive picture." Zelma retorted: "I don't, and some of my friends don't. . . . You have made a hussy out of me."

For an hour the two women talked it out. Marjorie tried to persuade Zelma to read *Cross Creek* before rushing to judgment. Zelma tossed the autographed book on a table, where it remained until her landlady later removed it. In the end, Marjorie believed she had appeased Zelma's anger. The two women embraced. Zelma thanked Marjorie for visiting the elderly Mrs. Cason in Island Grove. Marjorie left, confident "that we were on the old footing."

Marjorie's confidence was premature, as she discovered several months later. In November she decided to visit Zelma again, this time to give her a copy of *Cross Creek Cookery*. Accompanied by Idella Parker, her "perfect maid" of many years, Marjorie drove to Zelma's boardinghouse. Zelma came to the front door and glared at them stonily. "Oh, Zelma," Marjorie said enthusiastically, "here's a copy of my new book!" Zelma took the book, cursed, and threw it on the ground. "Don't you dare give that to me," she stormed.

Idella stooped down and picked up the book. "Come on, Idella," Marjorie said, and the two women left. Idella remembers that Marjorie was red-faced and very hurt, but she said nothing about Zelma on the way home. The next morning she asked Idella to bring her the copy of *Cross Creek Cookery* that Zelma had rejected. Marjorie opened the book and wrote: "For Idella. In memory of many happy hours together in the kitchen in Cross Creek. Marjorie Kinnan Rawlings. November 1942."

It didn't take long for Marjorie to discover just how angry she was. Two months later Zelma filed a lawsuit in the Alachua County Circuit Court, alleging that her reputation had been sullied and her privacy invaded by the Pulitzer Prize–winning author. Her lawsuit may have come as a shock, but it probably shouldn't have. Few people who knew this feisty and independent woman well were really surprised that it was Zelma Cason who broke from the friendly fold and aired her grievances in a court of law.

Chapter Two

My Friend Zelma

Zelma Cason was at the same time the least likely and the most likely person to sue one of America's most celebrated authors. Least likely in that she had been among Marjorie's closest friends and supporters, the one who had first introduced Marjorie to Florida and accompanied her on fact-gathering excursions in the cracker countryside. Most likely in that her volatile temper and feelings of estrangement from Marjorie created a powder keg of resentment; the goading of friends after *Cross Creek* was published lit the fuse of her discontent.

Zelma was born in Ziegler, Georgia, on May 29, 1890. Zelma's age was her particular vanity. For years she misstated it, even altering her birth date in the family Bible from 1890 to 1892. In her declaration (the legal pleading that initiated the lawsuit), Zelma listed her age as forty-six, when in fact she was nearly fifty-three. At the trial, under oath, she falsely testified that she was born in 1893. It seems that once Zelma Cason made up her mind about something, even the specter of perjury couldn't change it.

Zelma's mother was a "Zeagler," after whose relations Zelma's birthplace was named. Mrs. Cason had traveled to Georgia to be with her family during the birth, and she returned to Island Grove when Zelma was three weeks old. This tiny town four miles southeast of Cross Creek, the "village" as Marjorie termed it in her writings, would remain Zelma's home for most of her life.

Zelma's parents had come to Island Grove in the late 1800s. Her father was stationmaster on the railroad, and

Marjorie and Zelma take the census

the family lived in a comfortable house immediately east of the tracks. The house burned down after Mr. Cason's death in 1908, and the family moved to an adjacent house. Zelma had an older brother, T. Z., born in 1886, and a younger brother, born in 1893, who died at the age of five.

When asked at the trial to describe her life in Island Grove, Zelma responded with uncharacteristic brevity: "I lived as an ordinary person in the town of Island Grove; attended school there, and the East Florida Seminary, and matriculated in the State College for Women." Zelma's modest description of her early history was probably intended to counteract the defense claim that she was a well-known and outspoken personality. Other than enjoying an occasional horseback ride, she declared, her girlhood was uneventful and differed little from other girls her age. And as for her position in society, "[t]here was no society to move in in Island Grove."

Zelma's life after girlhood was that of "an average American citizen." She was not regularly employed for the first forty years of her life, though she did help T. Z. manage his orange grove and had a brief stint as census taker in 1930, a position that Charles Rawlings helped her to secure. From 1933 to 1935 Zelma worked for the Federal Emergency Relief Administration, first as the operator of a small nursery school in Island Grove, then as an investigative case worker in Gainesville. In 1935 she joined the Florida State Welfare Board as an intake visitor, whose duties included investigation and certification of old-age assistance, disability, and dependent children cases. She remained in this position, working out of Palatka and St. Augustine, until her retirement. During this time she maintained rooms in other towns and returned most weekends to Island Grove.

Her modesty at the trial notwithstanding, Zelma was an active citizen of whatever community she lived in. She was a member of the Island Grove and Palatka

Parent-Teachers Associations, the Red Cross, and the Florida and St. Johns County Social Workers' Association. She was a Worthy Matron of the Island Grove Eastern Star and a precinct inspector for the Democratic party. Zelma was also a property holder, owning eighty acres of land in Alachua County and some rental property in Island Grove.

The rental property was leased for a time to the Red Derby, a so-called "juke joint" where beer and soft drinks were sold. Marjorie hoped to make an issue of the juke joint at the trial to counter Zelma's claim that she was an unobtrusive citizen of Island Grove. Marjorie's lawyer obtained a written statement from the proprietor of the Red Derby, describing a "partnership arrangement" with Zelma and revealing that Zelma herself had paid for the beer license. But cooler heads prevailed, and the defense decided not to use this information at the trial. The proprietor was subsequently called to testify about Zelma's profanity; the juke joint was not mentioned.

By all accounts Zelma was a strong-willed, voluble, and opinionated woman. In a classic understatement she once admitted of herself: "When I'm interested in a particular question or matter I generally form an opinion about it which I don't change without good reason." Although one of the witnesses at the trial, a former member of the Florida State Welfare Board, would generously remember her as "a very charmingly outspoken person," an earthier Zelma is ingrained in the memory of those who knew her best.

Neighbor Snow Slater, himself a character in *Cross Creek*, described Zelma's clamorous behavior: "You could hear Miss Cason cussing for a quarter of a mile," he declared. "She was a small woman, maybe five feet four inches, but she cussed in a loud voice. She didn't care who heard her." Another neighbor, J. T. Glisson, had a similar memory: "If Miss Cason was in the local grocery store you would be aware of her profanity," he said. "She was very personable, and spicy as a whip." Years after the trial, lawyer Sigsbee Scruggs was asked to describe the woman he opposed. Zelma, he said fondly, was "as helpful and friendly a woman as you've ever seen, but she was entirely profane. That profanity was not an immorality—it was a habit with her!"

Zelma's niece, Clare Hadley, remembers her Aunt Zelma with affection:

> She was really a little five foot tall, busty, feisty female. And she was a social worker, and most of her clients adored her, and the ones who didn't hated her with a passion. And there was really very little if any in-between with people's feelings toward her. She had been very popular as a young girl. She was still dating when I was old enough to date, and was proposed, but no man was good enough in her eyes.

For all her noisiness, Zelma was a petite woman, "a tiny Dresden doll," as one acquaintance described her. At heart she was a homebody, and one of her great loves was cooking. She made a few good women friends, including Marjorie and Mae DuPree of nearby Citra, although she clearly preferred the company of men. Her great weakness—if this questionable adjective can be applied to such a stalwart figure—was an excess of feminine vanity. As Marjorie regretfully discovered, it was no compliment to that fragile ego to speculate whether Zelma "should have been a man or a mother."

But it was hard to ignore Zelma's masculine leanings. She wore pants at every possible opportunity, taught her niece and nephew to shoot, and enjoyed an occasional boxing match. And she was not above a show of violence if it suited her purposes. Zelma's niece recalls a time when the county was going to remove some trees near the Cason home. Zelma picked up her gun "and told them to get off her property or she'd shoot them." The men, quite certain that Zelma Cason meant what she said, left off their work.

Zelma had an active sense of humor, but she did not like to be teased or have attention drawn to her. She especially hated to be photographed. At the trial she testified that she seldom had her picture taken because "I so seriously objected to it." Her most recent photograph (aside from a World War II passport photo required to cross the St. Augustine bridge) had been taken at the age of fifteen. Even then, "I acted ugly when they took [it], because I didn't want my picture taken." Whether through vanity or anger, Zelma later destroyed almost all of the few photographs of her that remained.

Zelma's strategy at the trial was to portray herself as a private and demure personality, indistinguishable from other citizens of Island Grove. In the declaration she described herself as living "a quiet and normal life, seeking neither notoriety, fame nor publicity [and] avoiding . . . all conduct and behavior that would or might make her conspicuous." Though admitting to an occasional invective, Zelma denied that she was temperamental or in any way resembled Marjorie's "profane friend Zelma."

But Zelma's temper and tongue were legendary, and the defense enthusiastically summoned witnesses to both. Island Grove's deputy sheriff, whom Zelma had called a "son-of-a-bitch" in the heat of a political campaign, described her as a woman who liked to "ruin or rule." A Cross Creek fish merchant testified that Zelma tried to rent a fishing boat with the memorable words: "I want to catch me some God damn fish." A St. Augustine attorney told the jury that Zelma gave him "quite a blessing out" on the courthouse steps over a case involving the State Welfare Board.

One of the funnier incidents was related by Marjorie's friend Dessie Smith, whom Zelma heartily disliked.

Dessie often visited the Creek to go fishing with her uncle, Tom Morrison, and she always passed Zelma's house in Island Grove in the wee hours of the morning. On such occasions she couldn't resist tormenting Zelma by blowing her roadster horn. One morning at 4:30 Zelma's temper snapped, and she retaliated by calling out the game warden. Dessie described the scene to the jury:

> [W]e hadn't been out [fishing] but a few minutes when Miss Cason and a game warden came in a speed boat and circled by us a while and waited until we started in and followed us closely; and when we got in the game warden checked my license and the catch, which, fortunately, happened to be all right.

It was probably inevitable that Marjorie would gravitate to such a colorful and exciting personality. Zelma Cason was a real character, just the one to nose out other interesting characters and adventures. She was an appealing companion for a budding author, and Marjorie took to her from their first meeting.

Zelma was interested in Marjorie's writing, and she took pride in introducing Marjorie to the local scene. They saw each other almost daily, visiting in each other's homes, hunting, fishing, and picnicking. At the trial both women described their friendship as "intimate"; another witness testified that the two were "like sisters more than anything else."

At some point in the early 1930s, the friendship suffered a serious setback. Zelma told the jury that the breach occurred in March or April of 1931, when she met Marjorie in front of the Island Grove post office. Zelma had just returned from her uncle's funeral in Georgia. "My dear," Marjorie said. "I am so glad to see you back." "Don't you 'my dear' me," retorted Zelma. And she proceeded to accuse Marjorie of spreading gossip during her absence: "You told [my family] that some man should take me down across his knees and give me a good spanking for my little red flannel tongue. . . . [I'm] through with [you] for life!"

Marjorie was used to Zelma's moodiness, and she assumed that her temperamental friend would soon cool down. She tried to visit Zelma twice in Island Grove, but Zelma wasn't at home. Marjorie also wrote a conciliatory letter, believing that "the only way to soothe her ruffled feathers was to take the blame for everything, to apologize for things I had not even done." But to no avail. As far as Zelma was concerned, the friendship was finished.

Marjorie's explanation of the rift was somewhat different from Zelma's testimony. In January of 1931 Marjorie was convalescing from an operation at a cottage in St. Augustine. Zelma was with her. At the end of their stay, Zelma tried to persuade Marjorie to break off her friendships with fishing buddy Fred Tompkins and Zelma's nemesis, Dessie Smith. Marjorie refused, and Zelma was furious. While Zelma was in Georgia, Marjorie asked Mrs. Cason and T. Z. to convince Zelma she was being unreasonable. The confrontation at the post office occurred when Zelma returned. Marjorie denied making the "little red flannel tongue" remark.

Marjorie knew the degree of intimacy had changed, but she didn't consider the friendship with Zelma over. Instead, she blamed other circumstances for the emotional distance between them. The unmarried Rawlings brothers had left Florida, and "my lonely life at the Creek did not hold the same attractions for her." Zelma's disapproval of Fred Tompkins and Dessie Smith, with whom Marjorie spent a great deal of time, also tended to separate them. And in 1933 Zelma's work began to take her away from Island Grove. The frequent picnics and hunting parties stopped. Marjorie saw Zelma occasionally when she visited Mother Cason, and at rare intervals Zelma stopped at Cross Creek. "[W]e were always glad to see each other when we met," Marjorie insisted.

Despite Marjorie's optimism, the friendship deteriorated. Zelma had less and less contact with Marjorie's life and writings. She no longer escorted Marjorie through the countryside or brought her choice tidbits for her stories. Thus, the stage was set for the central controversy in the lawsuit—whether Zelma consented to have her story told in *Cross Creek*. If she had, she could not recover for invasion of privacy.

Zelma, of course, claimed that she had not consented. In her trial testimony she insisted that Marjorie had joined her on the census trip only "for the fun of it." She had never intended to help Marjorie gather material for her books. Still less did she mean to expose her own carefully guarded life to the reading public's scrutiny.

Marjorie's testimony on this point was considerably different. The Zelma of her memory was an eager contributor to the aspiring writer's store of information. Zelma "knew that I was a writer and seemed to be very much interested in my career," she testified. Two of the sketches in "Cracker Chidlings" were based on stories Zelma had told her, and Marjorie was forced to reject others as "unsuitable and perhaps distressing." One such story was deleted from the first draft of "The Census." An important if secondary reason that Zelma invited her on the census-taking trip, Marjorie maintained, was to gather material for her writings.

But Zelma's eagerness to lead Marjorie to other story subjects didn't necessarily mean that she considered herself suitable literary material. After the publication of *South Moon Under*, based on the life of their mutual friend Leonard Fiddia, Zelma remarked: "Marge, don't write a book about *me*." To which Marjorie laughingly replied, "Oh, I can't promise that."

At the time Marjorie took this to be false modesty. She explained to her lawyer: "Now . . . knowing her vanity, I took it as I take so many coy comments from women particularly. Perfect strangers say to me at gatherings, 'Don't you write about me,' when what they mean is that they would give their eye-teeth to be written about."

Marjorie gave a similar reason at the trial for ignoring Zelma's protest: "We were friends; and in my long experience as a writer I have invariably known the friends of writers to be pleased in the mention of them in a book, or story, or an article."

Marjorie plainly miscalculated in not seeking Zelma's approval. She may have been testing the waters when she told T. Z. Cason in 1941 that she was working on a new book: "[I]t is my life at the Creek, and you are in it and we are all in it." Marjorie probably suspected this would get back to Zelma, and better to let the more sympathetic T. Z. break the news. If confronted directly with the question "Can I write about you?", Zelma was bound to answer with a resounding "No!" And, frankly, Zelma was just too engaging a character to leave out of the book.

So *Cross Creek* went to press with Zelma in it.

And Zelma Cason went to war.

Chapter Three

A Declaration of War

Kate Walton of Palatka was a stand-out among Florida women in the early 1940s. At a time in the state's history when women were still treated as second-class citizens by the law, Kate, or "Miss Kate" as she was sometimes known, was a dedicated and versatile lawyer. Nor was she content to take a back seat to others of her profession and remain safely tucked away in the comforts of an office practice. Kate was primarily a litigator, with a large array of criminal and civil clients. Although at heart a shy and private person, she was an aggressive advocate of her clients' interests in the courtroom. Whether defending an accused murderer or suing a railroad for poisoning a farmer's cows, Kate Walton was at her creative best when trying cases before the all-male juries of her time.

Kate was born in Palatka on February 5, 1913, the second of four daughters. She decided to pursue a career in law, like her much-admired father, J. V. Walton. J. V. (the "J." stood for "Judge," his real name) graduated from Washington and Lee Law School in 1905 at the age of twenty-one. He soon developed a large practice in northern Florida, at a time when Palatka's position on the St. Johns River made it a major shipping port. He was disappointed in his ambition to be appointed state attorney because of pressure from the Ku Klux Klan, whose growing power he opposed, and he sometimes carried a gun because of Klan threats on his life. A newspaper account of the *Cross Creek* trial offered a rather folksy description of this sophisticated man: "Walton's mannerisms are as back country as a dish of collard greens, grits and side meat. But so have been the mannerisms of some very smart attorneys—the great Clarence Darrow among them." J.V. Walton was one of Florida's most prominent attorneys, and his Palatka practice was securely established when daughter Kate joined the fold.

Kate received her undergraduate degree from Florida State College for Women (now Florida State University) and enrolled in the University of Florida Law School in 1933. She received her best grades in such esoteric subjects as Roman law and admiralty law; she received only average grades in criminal law and trial practice, areas she would excel in as a practicing lawyer. Kate graduated from law school in 1936 and joined the Walton firm the same day. She was one of the first five women admitted to the Florida Bar and the first woman to practice law in Putnam County. In 1952 she married Frederick Engelken, a retired director of the U.S. Mint thirty years her senior. She maintained a private practice in Palatka for nearly fifty years, until forced by illness to retire shortly before her death in 1985.

Kate's nephew, William Townsend, who now practices law with the Walton firm, remembers his aunt with admiration:

She graduated [from law school] in the morning and was working that afternoon with my grandfather. She was always extremely close to him. He always wanted a son and never had one.

It gives me chills to think what it must have been like for a woman, back then. She never complained about it. She said that someone told her after she got started that "they won't take you as seriously, but they'll have to listen to you more politely. You'll have to play on that." And she developed a kind of style where she spoke slowly and to the point.

Kate encountered sexual discrimination in those early days, but she handled it with equanimity. She explained to her nephew that "everybody operates under disabilities." Attorney Parks Carmichael, Sigsbee Scruggs's law partner, often opposed Kate in the courtroom. "Kate asked really no favors because she was a woman," he recalled, "either of the juries or of other counsel or the judges." Kate even had to prove herself to her father. "Father didn't actually approve of women in law," admitted Kate's sister, Mrs. Lois Townsend. "But she made a believer out of him."

Kate was an intensely private person. Her penchant for privacy stood out particularly during the *Cross Creek* trial. Marjorie heard reports that Kate was "a fanatic on the question of invasion of privacy." To her death Kate refused to talk publicly about the case, maintaining a wall of silence in striking contrast to the boisterous press reports of the time. Kate's obituary in the local newspaper remembered her as "an essentially private person" and a "one-woman legal aid society" who generously helped many indigent clients without pay. She worked tirelessly for her clients, both at the office and at home. Kate may have jealously guarded her private persona, but her public one was given freely.

Stephen Boyles, who joined the Walton firm after Kate had been practicing almost thirty years, was struck by this dichotomy in Kate's nature. Kate was "an extraordinarily shy person" in her personal life, he observed, but "a tenacious, aggressive trial lawyer. She was a bulldog. When she latched on, there was no turning loose." Kate's outstanding characteristic as a lawyer was her inventiveness. "She would look at a situation and come up with a whole new way of approaching it," Boyles recalled. This quality of inventiveness would serve Kate well in Zelma Cason's unusual lawsuit.

No one will ever know just why Zelma decided to sue, or how she and Kate Walton came to join forces. Those

Zelma consults with her lawyer

in a position to know—Zelma Cason, Kate Walton, and J. V. Walton—are gone now, and their stories with them. As with any great trial drama, legends abound concerning the principal actors and their motives. Contradictory stories still circulate about the reasons the lawsuit was filed. But common threads of truth are woven throughout the various accounts, and some plausible answers can be pieced together.

Zelma herself gave some important clues to her motives in her trial testimony. After the publication of *Cross Creek*, she testified, she was provoked by friends and strangers alike. She first learned that she had been depicted in the book when she walked into her St. Augustine office and was teased by co-workers: "They began calling me 'Cross Creek,' and asked where my gun was that I have hooked to my side; and things like that." Was she, as Marjorie had written, "a man or a mother"? And would Zelma be willing to display some of her "famous profanity" for them? Zelma claimed that she received letters from all over the country, inquiring about her and asking whether she had been paid for the use of her name. Strangers pointed at her and approached her in restaurants. "I got to the place I would rather drive up to a pig stand and eat in my car," she complained.

This attention probably aggravated Zelma's resentment toward Marjorie, which had festered during the last few years of their relationship. "I thought [Marjorie] was a friend of mine, a very good friend," Zelma told the jury. "I think now she was not. . . . She was merely using me as a tool." And Zelma bristled at Marjorie's continuing friendship with Dessie Smith. The flattering portrayal of Dessie in *Cross Creek* was just one more slap in the face. Marjorie referred to Zelma's jealousy in a letter to her lawyer: "If I had written untrue paeans of praise [about Zelma], calling her a saint on earth, and had *at the same time* drawn an unfavorable picture of Dessie, whom she hates and of whom she has always been jealous, she would have gone up and down the land urging everyone to read 'Cross Creek.' "

Zelma also believed that Marjorie had profited at her expense. It was bad enough to be publicly laughed at; it was even worse to watch Marjorie reap the not inconsiderable financial gains. One defense witness, Mae DuPree, testified that Zelma told her Marjorie had "paid off" all the other *Cross Creek* characters except her. Ida Tarrant of St. Augustine, Charles Rawlings's great-aunt by marriage, testified that she was riding in a car with Zelma before the lawsuit when she noticed some law books on the back seat. When she asked what they were for, Zelma replied that she was going to sue Marjorie for slander. "I am going to get some of that easy money," she declared. Zelma herself testified that filing the lawsuit would prove to the world that "I didn't approve [of the book] and had not received anything from it."

Marjorie was hurt and confused by the lawsuit, and she speculated repeatedly about Zelma's motives, usually in letters to her attorney, Phil May. Her views on the subject changed as the suit progressed. She sometimes blamed Zelma's greed and vanity; at other times she blamed people who she felt had influenced Zelma. A few days after the lawsuit commenced in January of 1943, Marjorie wrote to May that Zelma was acting "from a combination of exhibitionism, greed, jealousy and venom." A few weeks later she wrote: "I thought in the beginning that poor Zelma's reaction was one of exhibitionism and venom, but as I read the declaration, I think that the hope of 'collecting' is the main motive." Two months later she speculated that Zelma was "definitely a paranoiac."

As the suit dragged on, Marjorie's anger intensified. In May of 1943 she wrote to Phil May that Zelma "is truly an evil and vicious person . . . she has devoted her life to making trouble." In October she theorized that Zelma was "motivated by greed and envy." By 1945 Marjorie had begun to blame Kate Walton, believing that she was impelled by publicity-seeking or gain. She laid a similar charge at the feet of Zelma's brother, T. Z., from whom Marjorie was now estranged. She wrote bitterly: "Somehow there seems to be a picture of the greedy son and daughter, who, under the aegis of an even greedier lawyer, avid not only for money but for personal publicity, are hoping to get money out of a family friend." At the same time Marjorie felt that Zelma's mother was on her side. "Under all circumstances ... Mrs. Cason is to be protected in the trial," Marjorie instructed her attorney. "She is a *genuine* friend and must not be hurt or embarrassed."

It's no wonder that Marjorie was confused about Zelma's motives. Rumors about the case were spreading like wildfire in the tinder-dry forest of community opinion. A friend wrote to Marjorie shortly after the suit was filed:

There is one rumor that it is blackmail and another rumor that Zelma quarreled with you a year before the book was published and she thinks that you published her statements to hurt her deliberately and she is using this method for revenge. There is another rumor that she is jealous and another rumor that her brother, Dr. Cason, instigated the whole thing because he was annoyed.

Perhaps many motives combined to fire Zelma's indignation. She was already angry at Marjorie and possibly envious of her success. Her aversion to public scrutiny was offended by Marjorie's humorous sketch. Goaded by friends, pestered by strangers, and spurred on by the realization that Marjorie would profit mightily by her embarrassment, Zelma either proposed a lawsuit or stumbled rather naturally into one.

Whether the lawsuit was indeed purposeful or was

urged upon Zelma by someone else is one of the most perplexing questions in this enigmatic case. Despite her claims to the contrary, Zelma was not initially disturbed by her notoriety in *Cross Creek*. Phil May learned during the trial from an unnamed source—too late to subpoena witnesses—that shortly after the book's publication Zelma appeared at the office of the State Welfare Board in Palatka "beaming with pride." Zelma talked about the book with her fellow employees. She continued the discussion over lunch with her supervisor. May assigned an investigator to interview the man, and he recalled that Zelma was flattered by the attention: "She was *not* displeased, and made *no* remark to the effect that she was displeased. I gathered the impression at that time that she was pleased to have been mentioned—she was all smiles."

At some point, however, Zelma turned peevish. She was not one to take teasing well, and certainly not for long. The seeds of litigation may have been planted (or at least nurtured) by a woman with whom Zelma boarded in Palatka. After reading the book the woman telephoned Zelma and angrily complained about the "definitely offensive" description. She explained to the jury: "I called Miss Cason at the office and told her I had read the book which she had procured for me and told her that if that were I, I really would do something about it."

When asked at the trial when she first decided to bring her lawsuit, Zelma evaded a direct answer. She intimated, however, that her decision was fixed by the time Marjorie brought her an autographed copy of *Cross Creek* in April of 1942, within two months of the book's publication. When Marjorie handed Zelma the book, "I told her that she would be sorry." Under cross-examination Zelma claimed that she could not recall when she first consulted an attorney, but it was sometime after she had read the offending passages.

Zelma's brother, Dr. T. Z. Cason, testified that Zelma spoke with him three times about a lawsuit. The first two times he was "very emphatic with her and advised her ... not to do it." The third time he told her that she would have to proceed without his advice, if she was still so determined.

Zelma was still so determined. And sometime after her confrontation with Marjorie she joined forces with an equally determined lawyer. Within months their determination ripened into action. Just how Zelma and Kate Walton came together has been—and continues to be—the subject of intense speculation. Kate herself did nothing to dispel the popular stories about her role in the case, maintaining an impenetrable silence amidst the rumors.

Perhaps fostered by this silence, the theory has tenaciously persisted that Kate initiated the contact, thinking it would be the basis for an interesting case. This theory was apparently fed by a remark attributed to Zelma. Mae DuPree, a friend of both Zelma and Marjorie, testified that Zelma told her: "It is not my case, it is a lawyer's case, and I don't know anything about it. They asked me if they could use my name to see whether an author could use a person's name in a book." In rebuttal testimony, Zelma emphatically denied making this remark.

Several stories still circulate concerning the origin of the lawsuit. One of them came from Sigsbee Scruggs, the colorful Gainesville lawyer who assisted Phil May in Marjorie's defense. His version of how Kate and Zelma met was recounted in a taped interview thirty years after the *Cross Creek* trial:

> Kate Walton went to Jacksonville to be operated on by Dr. Cason. While she was in her room in the hospital, Cason came in to see her one day, and she said, "Doctor, why don't Zelma ... sue Marjorie

Rawlings for invasion of privacy?" And Dr. Cason said, "What's that?" And she explained invasion of privacy to [him]. Dr. Cason told Zelma, and Zelma went to see Kate. That's the reason Kate handled the case.

Norton Baskin, who married Marjorie in 1941, tells a similar story about the lawsuit's origin:

Kate Walton, the lawyer, had been in [Riverside Hospital], and she'd had a very unusual, strange abdominal operation, and she was recovering from it, and [Dr. Cason] was so proud of it that three or four times a day he would walk in with three or four people and tell them about this and pull the covers back and say this is what we did. After five times of that Ms. Walton got enough of it and she said: "Look, you do that one more time and you got a suit on your hands." And he said, "For what"? And she said, "Invasion of privacy." So when Zelma decided she wanted to sue, Dr. Cason remembered Kate Walton.

This was the version of the story that Marjorie had heard. She alluded to it in a letter written to her attorney in January of 1944: "I feel that Kate Walton was wrong in objecting to Dr. Cason's bringing in of other doctors for certainly science comes ahead of any personal fussiness."

Clare Hadley, Zelma's niece, learned a different story from Zelma:

Zelma had been assigned to the Palatka area. First she was at Gainesville, and then Palatka as a social worker. And then she was sent to St. Augustine. But she was back in Palatka and having lunch with some friends, and someone said there was a lawyer there who'd like to meet her, that she felt she had a case against Marge Rawlings for what she'd said about her in the book. And so Kate was introduced to her, and talked her into the idea of a lawsuit.

Mrs. Hadley reports that she heard a similar account in talks with her father, Dr. T. Z. Cason, and Zelma's lawyers.

William Townsend was one of the few people with whom his aunt, Kate Walton, broke her silence about the case. Based on his discussions with Kate and with his grandfather, J. V. Walton, Mr. Townsend related the following account of how Kate and Zelma met:

Zelma came to her, but I think Zelma had gone to some other lawyers first, around in Gainesville and in the area. And [Kate] had had some experience in libel and slander actions at that time. Zelma's approach was that the matter was false, that she was not profane. However the facts [did not] bear out that interpretation. So when [Kate] first talked to [J. V. Walton] about it, he wasn't interested. Katy could do whatever she wanted to but [J. V.] was not interested. So she started working on the privacy angle. She was very original, very good mind. And after she came up with the idea, [J. V.] became interested.

Kate told her nephew that Zelma had come to her determined to file a libel action. Kate tried to talk her out of it, because she believed it would be difficult to prove that Marjorie's description of Zelma was false, as required by libel law. But Zelma insisted on a lawsuit, declaring that Marjorie had abused their friendship and *Cross Creek* was "the last straw." Kate then considered the possibility of an action for invasion of privacy and, concluding that it had merit, agreed to take Zelma's case. The trial record contains some additional clues about

Zelma's and Kate's association. Zelma was asked during cross-examination which lawyer she first consulted. She replied: "Miss Walton, in Palatka." Zelma's brother, Dr. Cason, was asked whether Kate Walton had been a patient at his hospital (in Jacksonville) prior to the filing of the lawsuit. He responded that she had, in 1939 or 1940.

Although the popular stories about the lawsuit's origin are very different, there are common elements that unite them: Zelma's inclination to take legal action, Kate's originality as a lawyer, and Dr. Cason's role in bringing the two women together. These elements, aided by parts of the trial record, can be pieced together to form a broad but credible account of how Kate and Zelma joined forces.

All the evidence suggests that Zelma was actively considering a lawsuit within a short time after the publication of *Cross Creek*. She spoke to her brother about it several times. Dr. Cason knew Kate Walton as a patient at Riverside Hospital (although he was not a surgeon, as some of the stories had it). When it was obvious that Zelma's mind was made up, he probably mentioned Kate's name to her. Zelma talked to Kate in Palatka about a libel action. Kate persuaded Zelma that the libel claim was weak, and after some research she recommended that Zelma sue Marjorie for invasion of privacy. Zelma readily agreed.

Whatever the chronology, one thing is certain. Zelma Cason was too bright and too independent to be the unwilling dupe of an ambitious lawyer. Over two years after the lawsuit was filed, a young writer met Kate and Zelma frequently at the Walton beach cottage. The following year he vacationed near Marjorie, and he told her that the lawsuit had been a constant topic of conversation. Marjorie wrote to her attorney that the young man was unable to shed light on the question of who initiated the lawsuit, but he was convinced of Zelma's sincerity.

"Zelma was certainly not unwilling and was by no means made a victim of Kate's phobia," Marjorie reported. "Zelma was in it heart and soul." Kate's sister, who saw Zelma often at the Walton house in Palatka, confirms this report. "You could feel the fire in her," she recalls. "She was not just mad, she was hurt. She felt singled out by a celebrity."

In Kate Walton, Zelma found a lawyer whose pluck and resolve matched her own. And so they formed a remarkable alliance that would do legal battle for over five years. Their "declaration of war" was precisely that: the "declaration" under the old Florida common law system of pleading was the formal written statement of the plaintiff's case. A popular if euphemistic maxim about the intricate legal procedure of the time was: "Accuracy is the aim of common law pleading, and brevity its soul." But anyone familiar with this cumbersome procedure knew that "brevity" was the least of its virtues. The Florida Supreme Court in the second appeal of Zelma's case would fittingly describe the prolix paper battle as "warfare by pleading."

The skirmish began on January 8, 1943, with the filing of a "praecipe" in the Alachua County Circuit Court, requesting the clerk to order service of summons on the defendants. Zelma's eleven-page declaration was filed on February 1, within the thirty-day period required by court rule. Because a woman could not sue without joining her husband (a law changed by the passage of the New Married Woman's Emancipation Act later in 1943), the declaration identified the unwed Zelma Cason as "a femme sole." Marjorie and her husband, Norton Baskin, were joined as co-defendants, in accordance with the principle that a husband was jointly liable for the torts of his wife.

Zelma's declaration was in four "counts," or divisions, each containing a separate claim for relief and demanding damages of $100,000. The first count, occupying all of six pages, stated a claim for invasion of privacy. Until the events in question, the count alleged, Zelma had "lived a quiet and normal life, seeking neither notoriety, fame nor publicity." Zelma and Marjorie "were open in their talk together, shared their pleasures and their sorrows, and in tacit and mutual confidence, freely disclosed their thoughts each to the other." Marjorie then "willfully and maliciously" exposed facts about Zelma in *Cross Creek* that should have been protected by "the unwritten law of friendship." Marjorie had wrongfully exposed Zelma's private life, interfered with her "right to be let alone," and caused her name to become "a by-word in the minds of the vulgar."

The second count was also a claim for invasion of privacy, with the further allegation that Zelma had never commercially exploited her own name, and that Marjorie had acted without Zelma's "foreknowledge, consent or acquiescence." This count, with its reference to consent, would be the only one to survive the first Florida Supreme Court appeal.

The third count was a claim for libel, alleging that Zelma's good name and reputation were damaged by false and malicious references to her violent temper and profanity. It charged that Zelma had been "brought into public scandal, ridicule and obloquy" as a result of the publication.

The fourth and final count (in a claim prescient of today's "right of publicity") alleged that Marjorie had exploited Zelma's personality for her own financial gain and had been "unjustly enriched" at Zelma's expense. Zelma should therefore be entitled to share in the ill-gotten profits from the sale of *Cross Creek*.

The declaration was signed by Kate and J. V. Walton, Kate having persuaded her father to join in the lawsuit. J. V. would later assume the primary role at the trial, perhaps because of his local prominence, or perhaps because of concerns over the reaction of an all-male jury to

a female litigator. But J. V.'s role was decidedly secondary in the overall prosecution of the case. The declaration
bore Kate's creative and careful stamp, and was probably her sole work. J. V.'s name appeared under Kate's
on the last page of the declaration, signed in the same
hand, undoubtedly Kate's. Over the next five years Kate
would draft all correspondence, legal pleadings, and
briefs, taking care of the day-to-day details and leaving
the shining moments at the trial for her celebrated father.

Marjorie received advance warning that Zelma intended to file a lawsuit. When asked at the trial how she
first heard about the suit, Marjorie responded that she
had "heard something I didn't give much credence to
from Mrs. Tarrant" (Charles Rawlings's great-aunt). The
rumor was confirmed in January of 1943, when Marjorie
was served a summons from the court. She received a
copy of the declaration in early February.

Marjorie's immediate reaction to the lawsuit was char-
acteristically upbeat. After reading the declaration she
wrote to Phil May:

> I think the Declaration is one of the funniest docu-
> ments I have ever read in my life. I laughed out loud
> all by myself, which I seldom do. The particular
> grievances and the way they are phrased make me
> feel that our so-called "defense" is infinitely simpler
> than I expected.

Marjorie's bravado belied the anger and frustration
that lay ahead. Zelma Cason was not one to be taken
lightly. Marjorie would learn soon enough this was no
laughing matter.

Chapter Four

Warfare by Pleading

In her more candid moments, Marjorie revealed something of the anguish and astonishment she felt at Zelma's betrayal. Soon after the suit was filed she visited the Glisson family at Cross Creek. Tom Glisson said, "I understand Zelma is suing you." Marjorie's eyes filled with tears. Glisson's son, J. T., was surprised at her reaction: "This was the only time I'd ever seen her emotional in my life. She was devastated by the terrible thing that had happened to her and she was hurt. She was hurt, not mad."

Marjorie decided to confront Zelma and try to talk some sense into her. One Sunday she drove from St. Augustine, where she now spent most of her time, to the Creek. She ran into T. Z. Cason picking some fruit in the Big Hammock grove. The two friends embraced. T. Z. said, "Marge, whatever comes of this it must not interfere with our friendship." Marjorie told T. Z. that she was on her way to Island Grove to see Zelma. She asked him to join her there.

Marjorie went on to the Cason home in Island Grove and was greeted cordially by Zelma's mother. Zelma was in the kitchen, and she emerged twenty or thirty minutes later. She received Marjorie warmly and offered to show her some family pictures. T. Z. arrived soon after and maintained a diplomatic silence as the two women talked.

Marjorie finally got down to business. "Zelma," she said, "I would like to know what this thing is all about. . . . It is a complete puzzle to me." Zelma replied,

51

"You can talk to my lawyer." Marjorie wasn't satisfied with this answer. "I don't want to talk to your lawyer," she persisted. "You and I have been friends too long." "My lawyer warned me not to talk to you," Zelma repeated. "If that is the way it stands, all right," said Marjorie. "Goodbye." The door slammed shut behind her. Marjorie claimed later that she was not angry when she left. "Mrs. Cason's screen door bangs behind you as you go," she told the jury. "I certainly did not slam it."

If Marjorie was indeed angry, such public displays of frustration were rare. Most of her feelings were poured out privately to her close friend and attorney, Phil May. Their voluminous correspondence from 1943 to 1948 forms a remarkable record of the case. Marjorie was an astute, articulate client who made frequent suggestions concerning trial strategy, evidence, and possible witnesses. May was a conscientious, devoted attorney who sought to bolster Marjorie's spirits and preserve her creative genius. His performance at the trial would earn the praise of a *Miami Herald* reporter: "Philip May of Jacksonville [is] small ... physically but not mentally." Through May's tireless ministrations, his famous client was able to weather the legal storm ahead with remarkable equilibrium and humor.

Phil May took pride in his Florida cracker roots. He liked to remark that he came from the red clay hills of Gadsden County, one of eight children born to a Quincy pharmacist. He delighted in making speeches as a child, and he always knew that he would be a lawyer. After graduating from the University of Florida in 1911, May worked as a clerk for the Clyde Steamship Line in Jacksonville to earn money for law school. He received his law degree from the University of Florida in record time and clerked briefly for a Jacksonville law firm before joining the army in World War I. He then returned to Jacksonville and was taken into partnership by T. G. Crawford. Crawford and May maintained a highly respected partnership for over fifty years. When it finally dissolved, it was the oldest existing law partnership in Florida.

In one of the many ironies of this remarkable case, May met Marjorie through their mutual friend, T. Z. Cason. Both men were members of the "Mensheviks," a small group of erudite professionals who met quarterly to present papers on intellectual subjects. Marjorie later became an honorary member of the all-male group, and several meetings were held at Cross Creek. The lawsuit destroyed the friendship between T. Z. and May. T. Z. could not understand why May would take the case against his sister, and he felt badgered during his brief testimony at the trial. May, for his part, believed that T. Z. had encouraged Zelma to sue. After the trial the two men avoided all contact, although they were practically neighbors in Jacksonville.

On paper, May was the attorney for Norton Baskin only. May's law partner, T. G. Crawford, entered a formal appearance for Marjorie. However, from beginning to end the case was Phil May's, with Crawford giving only occasional advice.

The first matter to demand May's attention was the question of "venue"—the locale of the legal proceedings. Florida law required that a case be tried in the county where the defendants resided or where the injury complained of had occurred. Zelma claimed this was Alachua County, where Cross Creek was located. May hoped to show that she had chosen the wrong court in which to air her grievances.

Marjorie and Norton were living chiefly in St. Augustine, in a fine apartment atop Norton's Castle Warden Hotel and in their nearby beach cottage. Marjorie's visits to her beloved Cross Creek were less and less frequent. So in February of 1943 May filed a legal document challenging the lawfulness of the Alachua County venue. But he warned Marjorie that he was doubtful they would win on this point, since Marjorie had presented copies of the book to friends in the Cross Creek area.

Marjorie seemed unconcerned at the prospect of a trial in Gainesville, where the Alachua County Circuit Courthouse was located. She wrote to May:

> [E]xcept for the inconvenience to Norton of having to leave his work here to go to Gainesville, I think it really makes very little difference whether the case, if it does materialize, is before a Gainesville or a St. Augustine court. The only possible advantage would be that in St. Augustine a jury would be remote from local factions around Island Grove. If you secured an objectively-minded jury at Gainesville, it would be all the same.

Marjorie's indifference on the question was fortunate, because she lost this first legal skirmish. The court rejected May's challenge and ordered the trial to take place in Gainesville.

Marjorie was confident at this early stage in the proceedings of her ultimate vindication. Shortly after the suit was filed she wrote to Phil May: "[I]f the case actually comes to trial, I wish to prove her wrong." After reading Zelma's declaration she exuded confidence: "Aside from my witnesses . . . I know that my word would carry against hers, for I am a great believer in the recognizability of truth in the human face and voice." Still, she began to suggest possible witnesses and legal strategies to prepare for the unlikely event that Zelma's case might actually go to trial. May, for his part, was cautiously optimistic. He wrote Marjorie that he had some "apprehension" about Zelma's case, but that he nevertheless believed all four counts of the declaration would fail.

On February 26, 1943, May filed a pleading testing the legal soundness of Zelma's declaration. In it he argued that the declaration was "bad in substance": a fortyish, unmarried plaintiff could not be defamed by the term "ageless spinster," nor could anyone short of a religious apostle be libeled by reference to his or her profanity. The declaration, he urged, should be dismissed without trial.

The matter was set for hearing before Judge John A. H. Murphree. Two weeks before the hearing May sent Judge Murphree a copy of *Cross Creek*, informing him in a letter that "we believe the discussions will be facilitated by your reading of the book in advance of the hearing." Marjorie congratulated May on this stroke of genius: "Now you should have let me autograph the book tenderly to Judge Murphree! It was very smart of you to send him a copy."

Whether Judge Murphree took the time to read *Cross Creek* is unknown; what did follow, however, was decidedly favorable to its author. On April 20 Kate Walton and Phil May appeared before Judge Murphree in a three-hour hearing. Kate surprised May by relying principally on the invasion of privacy claim in arguing against dismissal of the case. May remained confident of victory on the privacy question. The State of Florida had not yet joined the small but growing number of states that recognized the existence of a "right of privacy" by judicial decision or statute. May wrote to Marjorie: "It does not appear likely to me that John Murphree, a youthful judge, would, in the very beginning of his career, undertake to establish an asserted principle of law which has been rarely recognized in a few states." As the summer dragged on with no decision, he blamed the long delay on the judge's wrestling with the third count of the declaration—the libel claim—which May felt was Zelma's strongest point.

On August 9 Judge Murphree finally handed down his ruling. May reported to Marjorie in a jubilant (and, in 1943, extravagant) telephone call that the judge had sustained their position entirely and dismissed Zelma's declaration. However, the judge had given Zelma fifteen days to file an amended declaration, and May expected that Zelma and Kate would "take another try at it."

But Kate Walton did the unexpected. Based on her legal research, she was confident that the invasion of privacy claim was valid. So she elected not to amend and to rely instead on the existing declaration. On September 1, 1943, Judge Murphree entered a final judgment in Marjorie's favor. On October 19, within the sixty-day period permitted for appeal, Kate filed a notice of appeal to the Florida Supreme Court.

May tried to keep Marjorie's spirits up at this new turn of events. Referring to the first bill for legal fees he had sent after the August victory, May wrote:

> Your apprehensions about the total cost probably persuading you to regret that you didn't settle are wholly unjustified. Remember the famous comment of—was it Charles Cotesworth Pinckney?— "Millions for defense but not one cent for tribute." Besides, young lady, think of the valuable advertising you are getting.

Marjorie responded that May's bill had been eminently reasonable, but she added ruefully: "The publicity the book is getting is not nearly sufficient to compensate for the unpleasantness and expense."

May immediately began work on his brief to the Florida Supreme Court. He offered to show Marjorie a draft version, but tried to temper her enthusiasm for playing the role of legal advisor: "Your thoughts have been helpful to me throughout the case, but as you are, naturally, not familiar with legal procedure, some of your suggestions are not appropriate." Marjorie was contrite about her meddling: "I must seem to you as a patient does to a doctor, when he asks if he hadn't better try this, that or the other remedy, and the doctor has the treatment all mapped out!" Still, Marjorie couldn't resist sharing her ideas, and many would later prove useful at the trial.

On December 27 Kate Walton filed a forty-two-page appellant's brief. The brief was forceful, articulate, and sometimes emotional. May appraised Kate's work in a letter to Marjorie: "It is an interesting and in some ways clever document, but it does not impress me as a persuasive argument to the Supreme Court on this record." May still felt that Zelma's libel claim was strongest, and he couldn't understand why Kate had covered it so "sketchily."

In fact, Kate used only four pages of the brief to argue the libel claim; the remaining pages were devoted to invasion of privacy. Kate believed (correctly, as time would prove) that the Florida Supreme Court was ready to recognize an individual's right of privacy, and she confronted the history-making nature of the case head-on. In the brief, she emphasized the growing acceptance of the law of privacy by other states. But she freely acknowledged that Zelma's case was unique: "It is readily admitted that no case has been found involving an invasion of the right of privacy in precisely the manner employed in the instant case." The court's decision, Kate urged, would greatly affect "the growth and development of our manners, customs and culture." For the right of privacy meant that every citizen, subject to reasonable laws and due regard for the rights of others, "has the positive right to be let alone."

Kate then turned from reason to emotion. Marjorie's "clever and scathing verbal description" had inflicted a "gross indignity" on the hapless Zelma Cason, "a gentlewoman ... of Georgia stock." This "impertinent intrusion" into Zelma's privacy was motivated solely by greed and power:

Defendant had no legal reason or excuse for thus violating plaintiff's right of privacy; she did it for money and self-aggrandizement. She betrayed her "friend Zelma" and exposed her to the jeers of the multitude for thirty pieces of silver.

Kate's own intense feelings about privacy may have stirred her to such heights of dramatic eloquence. This point was not lost on Marjorie, who wrote to May: "The tone of the brief ... would make one think that Kate Walton was trying her own case as well as Zelma's."

The ball was now in the defendants' court. Marjorie and May decided to meet to discuss the final draft of their appellee's brief. Plans to make an overnight visit to Cross Creek were canceled because of May's reluctance to take time away from his writing, and the two finally met in Jacksonville. The brief was filed on January 15, 1944. On February 3 May traveled to Tallahassee —without Marjorie—for the short oral argument before the Florida Supreme Court. Both J. V. and Kate Walton appeared on Zelma's behalf. The argument was heard by all members of the court, a circumstance indicating the importance of the case. Afterwards, May reported to Marjorie: "The argument went well, according to my lights, but of course I'm prejudiced." The Waltons were "completely overshadowed," he added confidently. Marjorie's reaction to the oral argument was uncharacteristically pious:

I thought about you all day on the third, and said an honest prayer. And did not get drunk. I agree with you that God is on our side, and that right is might, etc., for my motives were kindly and Zelma's (and T. Z.'s) were not.

But Marjorie's prayers were to no avail. On November 24, 1944, the Florida Supreme Court by a five-to-two vote reversed the judgment in Marjorie's favor and remanded the case to the Alachua County Circuit Court for trial. The court agreed with Judge Murphree's dismissal of Zelma's other three counts, but ruled that Zelma was entitled to her day in court on the privacy claim in the second count. For the first time in Florida history, the court (relying largely on authorities cited in Kate's brief) recognized invasion of privacy as a redressable civil wrong. "[T]here is a right of privacy, distinct in and of itself . . . for breach of which an action for damages will lie," the court declared.

In its opinion, the court acknowledged that Marjorie's depiction of Zelma was flattering:

> [O]n the whole she portrays plaintiff in a favorable light and evinces a real admiration for her. The quotations from the defendant's book . . . are on the whole complimentary and tend to create the impression that the author's friend Zelma was one who was worthy of her friendship—a fine, strong, rugged character,—a highly intelligent and efficient person, with a kind and sympathetic heart, and a keen sense of humor. . . . [T]he world would be better off if we had more Zelmas of the type so graphically pictured in "Cross Creek."

But flattery wasn't enough. The portrayal was also "a rather vivid and intimate character sketch." If Zelma had not consented to its publication, she was entitled to at least nominal damages.

It didn't matter, the court reasoned, that the description of Zelma was true. Nor did it matter if Marjorie had written it without malice. However, the right of privacy was not absolute. Balanced against it was the strong public interest in free speech. If Marjorie could prove that the publication involved a matter of "general or public interest," she would win the lawsuit. She would have to do this before a jury of her peers. Accordingly, the court sent the case back to Judge Murphree for trial.

May reported the "bad news" to Marjorie in a letter the next day. "You will get some academic comfort from Judge Brown's appraisement of your characterization of Zelma," he wrote, but "[t]he most comforting part ... is his statement that the value of 'Cross Creek' as a literary work and the interest of the public in it are defenses." Marjorie responded with a magnanimous press statement that she authorized May to release to the Associated Press:

> I feel that the opinions of both the concurring and the dissenting judges of the Supreme Court are entirely favorable, and that in voting for a trial of the case they have shown a great and proper justice in protecting the rights of any citizen to a public hearing of grievance, real or imagined. As to the ruling that the plaintiff has a reasonable case, unless the publication of "Cross Creek" is proved "warranted in public interest," I can only hope in all humility that anything I may ever have written about my beloved Florida is so warranted.

Though deeply disappointed, Marjorie echoed this generous appraisal of the court in her correspondence to May. "[The justices] evidently leaned over backward in their attempt to be fair, which is all right," she wrote. "I admire them for their fairness." Marjorie's high spirits about the case revived May's own flagging morale. He began work on a petition for rehearing, which he hoped would persuade the court to reverse its ruling. May and Marjorie discussed the petition over one of Marjorie's superb dinners at Cross Creek. But the Supreme Court was unmoved. On January 16, 1945, the petition for rehearing was denied.

Marjorie was faced with the inevitable prospect of a

trial. For two years she had actively considered her trial strategy, but somehow it had all seemed so distant and theoretical. The battle was fought with pleadings and motions, not with real people. Now the probability of an extended courtroom drama descended on her with full force.

Marjorie's first response was to hire a Gainesville attorney to assist May at the trial. Not that May needed any help in trying the case. But May and Marjorie decided that a Gainesville jury would be more sympathetic if one of their own local boys was sitting at the counsel table with big-city lawyer May. The choice was easy. For reputation, experience, emotional appeal, and sheer local color, no lawyer in Alachua County could touch the likes of one man—Sigsbee Lee Scruggs.

Marjorie and Norton arrive at the courthouse

Chapter Five

On to Courtroom Battle

Sigsbee Scruggs didn't come by his name in any ordinary way. Like the rest of his life, his appellation was singular and theatrically dramatic. Scruggs was an old English name, worn proudly for generations by such notables as Bubbles Scruggs, exotic dancer and early patron of Lloyd's of London. Sigsbee's ancestors left England to settle in the Carolinas, later moving to Georgia. Sigsbee's father migrated from there to northern Florida, where he was a farmer, storekeeper, and tax assessor. Sigsbee was born in Aucilla, Florida, in 1898. He was christened "Sigsbee" in honor of Captain Charles D. Sigsbee, Confederate war hero and commander of the battleship *Maine*. His unique and colorful name would carry him through a unique and colorful career.

Sigsbee's mother died when he was two, and his father remarried. At the age of twelve Sigsbee went to live with his older brother, Will, a school teacher. Sigsbee drove the wooden school wagon to help pay for his keep, and he accompanied the rhythmic clopping of horses' hooves with melodious bursts from his harmonica. At the age of sixteen Sigsbee finished the tenth grade, passed the state teacher's exam, and commenced teaching in the northern Florida communities of Wabassa and Bell. While teaching he met and married the daughter of a successful farmer. Sigsbee's father-in-law encouraged him to enter the University of Florida and helped to pay his expenses. It was only natural that the fast-talking, quick-witted Sigsbee, stand-out on the university debate team, would cap his undergraduate work with a law degree. He graduated from the University of Florida Law School in 1922. The next fifty-six years were devoted to the real love of his life—the practice of law.

Although Sigsbee was best known for his trial work, he began with a real estate practice in the office of another Gainesville attorney. He soon struck out on his own and began dabbling in real estate. He eventually set up several local subdivisions and parlayed his modest investments into higher-stakes land earnings. This gave him the financial freedom to practice law the way he wanted to—helping people no one else wanted to help, often without charge.

Sigsbee soon became known as a champion of the underdog, a lawyer who zealously defended blacks and poor dirt farmers. He once represented a farmer in Starke who had "borrowed" some expensive equipment to clear his land. Sigsbee successfully defended the man on a theft charge before a sympathetic jury of the man's neighbors. He gained special notoriety in the Cross Creek vicinity for his effective representation of cracker fishermen, who were engaged in constant warfare with the Florida State Game and Freshwater Fish Commission. Sigsbee explained his special relationship to Cross Creek in an interview late in his career:

> I have known the Creek since I began the practice of law in 1922. I represented approximately 70 percent of the people who lived there originally. There was many illegal fishermen, the same people that Marjorie talks about in her book, who fished with nets and traps, which was against the law. I defended all these people. Not some of them, but every one of them.

Sigsbee's success rate was so high that after his retirement the State asked him to defend some game wardens who were being sued by the fishermen they had arrested. Sigsbee agreed on the condition that he didn't have to do the work near Cross Creek, where his loyalty lay with the beleaguered fishermen. He won the civil suit for the State and successfully prosecuted criminal charges against the men. He was opposed in the criminal case by none other than Kate Walton.

Sigsbee's temper was almost as legendary as his trial record. He once defended a young man accused of murder in the small north Florida town of Trenton. The prosecution's star witness was the town marshal, whom Sigsbee "nailed to the wall" during cross-examination. A mistrial was declared in the case, and a new trial was scheduled in Gainesville. Between the two trials, Sigsbee and the marshal confronted each other on the main street in downtown Trenton. Sigsbee's son, Sigsbee Lee Scruggs, Jr., remembers the still-famous fight that followed:

[The marshal] came up to him in the middle of town and said, "I want to talk to you. I don't appreciate what you did." And Daddy said, "Listen, if you tell the truth, there won't be a problem. But if you go lie, I'm going to do the same thing I did to you before." And [the marshal] said, "I'll just have a little at you." And Daddy said, "That's fine with me."

And Daddy was 5'8", about 230 pounds, big-shouldered and heavy arms. Very powerful man. Quick though. So everybody gathered, and they went at it. They would fight for about twenty minutes and run out of breath. Daddy said he hit him with everything he could. But he couldn't knock him down. Two or three times they would stop and then they would go back and fight. And about the second time one of the fellas in town got between them and said, "You might as well quit this 'cause neither one of you can knock the other one down." So they quit.

Came back over here in the courtroom. [The marshal] got on the stand and lied again, and he nailed him again. Daddy's client was acquitted.

In addition to his criminal practice Sigsbee had a thriving divorce practice. He quickly developed a reputation for straightforward, no-nonsense "marriage counseling," and he was instrumental in saving many a foundering marriage. So effective was he that local ministers would send couples to him to counsel. Sigsbee "didn't mince any words," a tactic that apparently shocked the parties into marital sanity. As a youngster Sigsbee's son witnessed one of these "counseling" sessions and heard Sigsbee's unforgettable advice: "He said, 'Ma'am, I don't blame him for divorcing you. You're fat. You don't dress. You don't make yourself up. I'll bet you don't take a bath every day. Now why in the hell don't you do something about it?'"

Gainesville attorney Clara Gehan (who attended law school with Kate Walton) once found herself opposing Sigsbee in a bitter divorce suit. She represented the father in a hotly contested child custody battle, and during a recess in the proceedings the parties met in the hall. Ms. Gehan will never forget what followed:

Sigsbee turned to the young couple, and he said, "I want to tell you all something. Nobody can afford a divorce, particularly where there's children involved. And I know, because I'm a divorced man." And I'll be damned if they didn't go off, and ... came back and told the judge, "We're going to dismiss the case and reconcile."

Sigsbee quickly became known for his effective courtroom technique. No lawyer in Alachua County could match his skill in winning over local juries. Parks Carmichael, his law partner for forty years, attributed Sigsbee's success to his inquisitive mind: "Mr. Scruggs knew as much about human nature and as much about popular subjects as anybody that every lived. He was very convincing with a jury."

Sigsbee's magnetism didn't stem from his personal appearance. His son remembers him as "the world's worst dresser," who would "go into the courtroom looking like hell." In his five-dollar sports coat, he managed to woo the jury through persuasion and sheer art. He was particularly adept at selecting favorable jurors. His technique in the questioning of prospective jurors before trial (the so-called "voir dire") was to get one of them nodding agreement with him. He would then go on to the next juror until he, too, was nodding. "He said if he could get them nodding, he knew he had his case won," his son recalls.

It was Sigsbee's prowess with jurors that appealed to Marjorie and May. They judged, rightly, that there was no better man to help select a friendly jury. And Marjorie knew from experience that Sigsbee was a formidable figure in the courtroom. She had met him in that arena once before.

Several years earlier one of Marjorie's hired men, Samson, was shot by Henry, another Creek resident. Marjorie insisted that Henry be prosecuted for the offense. The rest of Cross Creek lined up solidly behind Henry. Old Boss Brice and Tom Glisson decided to hire the best lawyer in the county to defend Henry—Sigsbee Scruggs. Under pressure from her neighbors, Marjorie declined to give testimony at Henry's preliminary hearing. Sigsbee prevailed, and the charge against his client was dismissed.

Marjorie wrote about the incident in *Cross Creek*, although she didn't mention Sigsbee by name. But she never forgot him, and she still smarted from her humiliating surrender to community opinion. Common sense and the exigencies of Marjorie's situation prevailed over pride, however. When friends at the Creek strongly urged Marjorie to hire Sigsbee as local counsel, she readily agreed. She wrote to May: "[Sigsbee] is popular all over the county, is clever with juries, and has a large following in Island Grove and environs."

May wrote to Sigsbee on February 7, 1945, inviting him to assist in the case. Sigsbee wrote back that he was happy to help the defense, although he, too, had been asked to sue Marjorie over *Cross Creek:*

> I have watched, with much interest, the suit against Mrs. Baskin inasmuch as I knew all of the parties, and inasmuch as I, myself am one of the "characters" of the book. Also one of the other "characters" of the book approached me at one time about bringing suit. I refused upon the same legal basis as you are now defending.... Under these circumstances, I will be glad to assist you for reasons of interest as well as from a legal standpoint.

May and Marjorie were intrigued by the news that someone else had thought about suing, but nervous speculation about who it might be soon gave way to relief. "I believe that we have gone a long way towards obtaining a fairly united community support," May wrote Marjorie. "With Sigsbee in the case, we should have a valuable pipeline of information from Cross Creek."

May didn't need Sigsbee's help in formulating his defense strategy. He had already settled on a line of defense following the Florida Supreme Court's opinion. The court had ruled that the right of privacy did not prohibit publications involving matters of public interest. May therefore intended to prove that *Cross Creek* did involve such matters of public interest, for two reasons. First, the book was great literature, nothing short of a work of American folklore. Second, Zelma Cason had attained the status of "public figure" due to her community activities and meddlesome conduct.

These defenses were incorporated in the defendants' "pleas" (or formal responses) to Zelma's invasion-of-privacy count, filed by May on March 3, 1945. In the pleas May argued that Zelma had not lived a "quiet and private life," as she claimed. On the contrary, she was a public official in her capacity as census taker, worker in the Federal Emergency Relief Administration, and employee of the Florida State Welfare Board. She was also prominent in social, religious, and civic affairs, and was generally known as "a forthright, outspoken person of strong and definite convictions." Zelma had invited Marjorie to accompany her on the census-taking trip and had helped to gather material for Marjorie's writings. The fruit of these efforts—the critically acclaimed autobiography, *Cross Creek*—was itself a matter of "legitimate general public interest," insulating it from legal liability.

Kate Walton attacked these pleas with yet another legal pleading. On June 14 she and May argued their positions in a lengthy hearing before Judge Murphree. May reported to Marjorie that most of the time was consumed by Kate's impassioned argument:

> I gathered from Kate Walton's extended and embittered argument that she is a crusader, leading a group who are intent upon driving you from the State, so that you will not continue to besmirch Florida and its people with your sort of writing about Florida, and that she feels that autobiographies and biographies are not to be written unless the author pays all of the characters whom she portrays in the book.

Kate's argument was only a partial success. On August 14 Judge Murphree issued an order striking a number of the defendants' pleas as repetitive or without legal merit. But the substance of Marjorie's defense remained intact.

The defendants were given more time to file amended pleas, and a new round of attack and counterattack was begun, which occupied most of the remainder of 1945. Marjorie bemoaned the drawn-out paper war in a letter to May: "I suppose all this backing and filling about amendments and what not is necessary, but it seems goddam silly to a layman."

Marjorie continued her zealous interest in all phases of the litigation, a trait that was both helpful and trying to her patient lawyers. Among her more productive efforts during this period were contacts with potential witnesses. Marjorie smoothed ruffled feathers with friendly visits and autographed books, and she emerged with the Cross Creek community solidly on her side. Her efforts to discourage her lawyers from filing interrogatories (questions to be answered by Zelma under oath) were politely derailed, but Sigsbee later reported to May that Marjorie had won him over to a certain trial strategy during a particularly persuasive personal visit. Marjorie was never one to keep all her fingers out of the legal pie, as her lawyers were constantly reminded.

In the meantime Marjorie did not let the lawsuit interfere with her holiday cheer. One of the recipients of her seasonal good will was the elderly Mrs. Cason, Zelma's mother, whom Marjorie visited in Island Grove a few days before Christmas of 1945. She found Mrs. Cason bundled up against the bitter cold. Marjorie gave her a gift of whiskey, and Mrs. Cason suggested that they sit in the only warm room in the house—the bathroom. Marjorie related their odd encounter in a letter to May:

> I gave her the quart of Calvert's wrapped festively and she thanked me with real gratitude. . . . Mrs. Cason brought in two jelly glasses and we each poured generous measures. She sat on the toilet and I sat on a low stool and we enjoyed our drinks and a long chat. I said, "I was sorry not to get you your

Christmas liquor last year," and she said, "Marge, I understood."

We got expansive, and I said that my feeling for Zelma had never changed, that I should always feel the same affection, and that I felt that behind and beyond everything Zelma still loved me, too. I said that I blamed Kate Walton for the present mess. . . .

It does seem rather incongruous for a daughter to be sueing me for invasion of privacy, while her elderly mother sits on the john and drinks a half-jelly-glass of whiskey with me.

While Marjorie was carrying on with Christmas traditions, her lawyers began a new phase in their preparation for trial. They now made arrangements to take several depositions (sworn testimony of witnesses who would be unavailable for trial). The procedure was costly and time-consuming. In December of 1945 May went to New York to talk to several people at Charles Scribner's Sons, Marjorie's publisher, about their scheduled depositions.

May and Marjorie were both disappointed by Scribner's "ostrich attitude" about the case. Marjorie had expected her publisher to rally publicly and financially to her defense, especially since it was editor Max Perkins who had suggested that she write the extra paragraph describing Zelma. She was wrong on both counts. Scribner's, while supportive, remained very much in the background, and the firm did not offer to defray Marjorie's substantial legal costs.

Scribner's may have feared that it, too, would be sued as the publisher of *Cross Creek*. A hint of this concern surfaced in a letter from Charles Scribner to Marjorie shortly after she was served with notice of the lawsuit. Even if a nominal settlement could be made with Zelma, Scribner speculated, "this might be dangerous as everyone else whom you mention in the book might think that they could get a little money out of you by starting suit." The fear of additional litigation was not unfounded. May reported to Marjorie that he "intuitively gathered" from Kate Walton's remarks during an earlier hearing that she was considering filing a lawsuit against Scribner's in New York. Marjorie heard similar rumors from friends.

May wrote to Charles Scribner periodically to keep him abreast of the case and to urge him to keep track of any newspaper coverage, admonishing that "a successful termination of the suit against Mrs. Baskin will establish the security of your firm from attack." Scribner responded by sending news clippings from the *New York Times*, but he advised May that his company wanted to maintain a low profile and avoid publicity. After the Florida Supreme Court reversed the dismissal of Zelma's privacy claim, May felt that Scribner's cooperation was essential in preparing the public interest defense. He also believed that the New York depositions should be handled by Scribner's own lawyer, thus sparing Marjorie further expense.

On January 16, 1946, the depositions of seven defense witnesses, including Charles Scribner, Max Perkins, and Whitney Darrow of Scribner's, were taken in New York City. Although he would not be present, May had written the deponents a lengthy letter outlining the defense strategy. Marjorie was represented at the depositions by New York attorney Edward Perkins, brother of Max Perkins. Kate Walton made the long trip from Florida to question the witnesses. Afterwards, Perkins wrote to May that the depositions had gone well. Kate, he reported, had cross-examined the witnesses about financial receipts from the sales of *Cross Creek*, hoping to show that Marjorie had "made a pot of money" at Zelma's expense.

But if May and Marjorie counted on Scribner's picking up the tab for Edward Perkins's legal fees, they counted wrong. In March Marjorie received a bill from Perkins for $253.95. She complained to May:

> I feel that Scribner's is being very small indeed, in leaving it up to Mr. Edward Perkins to send me a personal bill. I am reasonably sure they must use his firm on a retaining basis, and it seems to me the least they could do was to "count me in." I think I shall write Charles Scribner, addressing him as "Dear Mr. Shylock Scribner."

Marjorie lost no time in writing to Charles Scribner. Upon receipt of the peppery letter, Scribner telephoned Edward Perkins. Perkins then wrote to May apologetically, explaining that he was not on retainer, that business manager Whitney Darrow had told him to send his bill directly to Marjorie, and that he had already reduced his normal legal fee. Marjorie promptly sent a check for $250.00 to Perkins, anticipating that he might refuse its tender. Instead, much to her chagrin, Perkins responded with a reminder that another $3.95 was due! Incredulous, Marjorie wrote to May:

> Well, the joke is on you. I laughed so, at the bill for $3.95, when you thought Mr. Edward Perkins was likely to return my check, with expressions of nobility and compliments all around. Then I thought, what the hell am *I* laughing about? The joke's on *me*. . . . I have sent Mr. Perkins his $3.95. Was so tempted to make it $3.98.

Marjorie had every reason to be concerned about money and to hope in vain that Scribner's would lend a hand. As the lawsuit lingered on her legal costs escalated dramatically. May's bills were infrequent (usually once a year) and eminently reasonable. Much of his work was done for a greatly reduced fee. "I feel that I am carrying a torch in this suit and wish that we could leave the question of compensation out," he apologized. But still the bills mounted. By March of 1946 Marjorie had spent nearly $2,500, and there was yet the cost of two attorneys at trial to consider. In June she complained to Max Perkins that her legal costs had ballooned to about $4,500, with some fees still unpaid. Although the exact figure is unknown, Marjorie's letters indicate that she spent close to $10,000 to defend the lawsuit, a considerable sum in the 1940s. Other sources place the figure much higher.

Marjorie could have avoided this expense. From the start it was obvious that the lawsuit could be settled for much less than it would cost to defend. But there was never a serious effort to do so. The reasons were both personal and professional, closely tied to the emotions generated by the suit and Marjorie's sense of duty as a writer.

From the very beginning Marjorie took an adamant stand against settlement of any kind. She wrote to May immediately upon learning of the lawsuit: "I should not be willing to buy [Zelma] off for a single worn dime, for the same reason that I would not be willing to 'soft soap' her. She is in the wrong." A few months later she rejected May's advice that the case could be readily settled. "Millions for defense but not one cent for tribute," she decreed.

May tried once more to encourage Marjorie to settle about a year after the suit was filed. He was deeply concerned that the case was draining Marjorie's creative energies, and he believed that a simple apology might persuade Zelma to lay down her arms. He implored Marjorie to settle in a heartfelt letter:

Your contributions to the world through what you are doing with your pen are of vastly more importance than the satisfaction you may eventually derive from a complete judicial victory over Zelma. Your talents give you such a heavy responsibility that your personal feelings must be sacrificed, if that is the price you have to pay for any impairment of the effectiveness of those wonderful gifts.

Marjorie replied with gratitude that May was a "true and loyal friend," but settlement (and in particular, an apology) was entirely out of the question: "I could not consider apologizing to Zelma under any conditions, for I feel I owe her none. . . . I should not consider settling with her for the same reason, for a single red cent." She also worried that settling with Zelma would encourage others to sue:

> [T]hat would lay me liable to paying off some of the other people, who are very friendly, but some of whom would at once pitch in with a suit or threat of their own if Zelma collected anything at all and broadcast it to the world, as she would do.

After her loss in the first Florida Supreme Court appeal, Marjorie's attitude toward settlement seemed to soften. She wrote to May that despite her certainty of "ultimate vindication," she would like to avoid trial for "two entirely unselfish and humanitarian reasons": the wish to avoid pitting neighbor against neighbor as witnesses, and the wish to save Zelma court costs. She also encouraged May to have a talk with Zelma's brother, T. Z., believing that he might persuade Zelma to drop the suit. Marjorie remained convinced that through some miracle Zelma would capitulate. She wrote to May one month before trial:

> I still say, that when I have not given in and offered to settle out of court before the suit goes to trial . . . they will call quits. . . . [I]t seems to me that

T. Z. must certainly wake up sometimes at night with the heebie-jeebies at the thought of the costs, if they lose. They cannot be *that* sure of winning.

The reasons for Marjorie's refusal to settle ran far deeper than stubborn pride or wounded friendship. She was convinced that the principle of artistic freedom was at stake in the lawsuit, and she felt duty-bound to defend the rights of all authors. Other writers kept track of the suit and encouraged Marjorie in her efforts, though none offered financial assistance. Marjorie's admirers included Margaret Mitchell of *Gone With the Wind* fame, who corresponded with Marjorie during this period. "Margaret Mitchell came across with a rush," Marjorie explained to May. "She adores law suits, and she feels that in the many court battles she has had, she is helping to protect all writers against hi-jackers." It's not surprising, then, that Marjorie felt settlement was out of the question. "I could not stop short of complete vindication where so vital a principle was at stake," she insisted.

For her part, Zelma seemed no more anxious to settle than Marjorie. Marjorie heard rumors a few weeks into the lawsuit that Zelma was willing to settle for $8,000. A mutual friend, Mrs. Grace Bugbee, reported that Zelma had come into her St. Augustine florist shop and mentioned the figure. But if this was true, the offer was never conveyed to Marjorie's lawyer. Zelma undoubtedly felt that she had a bone to pick and her own principle to vindicate. As a woman of strong opinions and obstinate nature, she was an unlikely candidate for settlement. Zelma's niece confirmed that her aunt never once thought of backing down: "Zelma loved a fight!"

So the war waged on, and the two camps prepared to do battle in a Gainesville courtroom. For three years Marjorie and Zelma circled each other at a distance, leaving the paper war to their lawyers. But one month before trial they met face-to-face, in an incident that Marjorie described to May as "so utterly weird . . . I would not be surprised if you threw up your hands and relinquished the whole damn case."

The meeting took place on April 16, 1946, five weeks before the start of the trial. Marjorie returned to her beach cottage near St. Augustine and found a note from Clare Hadley, Zelma's niece. The note said that Clare had stopped by in the hope of seeing Marjorie, and she was sorry to have missed her. Marjorie gathered up Norton and drove down to Clare's cottage, intending to invite her over for a visit. Marjorie described what happened next in an incredulous letter to May:

> We drove down, and since I was in a house-coat . . . Norton went up to the Spenser cottage to see Clare. She came down to the car, and said they were just about to eat supper, and we talked a bit, and then she said, "Please come on up and have a drink with us. There isn't a soul there but Aunt Zelma."
> Realizing that she must have called by my cottage with "Aunt Zelma's" knowledge, love nor money could not have kept me from going up for a drink. . . . So we went up, and I apologized for my house coat, and Zelma apologized for her bare feet, and we had a drink of whiskey. . . .
> Norton came away shaking his head. He said it just did not make sense for two women who were at each other's throats, to chat so amiably about Cason family matters, and I reminded him that I had never been at Zelma's throat, and was actually glad to see her, and she certainly seemed glad to see me. . . .
> Now the whole goddam business is ridiculous —.

But this strange respite from the legal hostilities didn't signal an end to the conflict. Witnesses were subpoenaed, jurors summoned, and final preparations made for the trial, which was scheduled to commence on May

20. During the first week of May, Norton whisked Marjorie off to Louisville for the Kentucky Derby to divert her attention from the coming ordeal. She came back refreshed, her resignation at the prospect of the trial turned to eager anticipation. She wrote an upbeat letter to May: "I see no reason why we couldn't have a whale of a good time."

As it turned out, the whole town of Gainesville would have a "whale of a good time." That usually sedate community would shortly be convulsed with a mad press of news reporters, curiosity seekers, and local celebrities. It was legal pageantry the likes of which the good citizens of Alachua County had never seen—and would not soon forget.

Chapter Six

The *Cross Creek* Trial

On Monday morning, May 20, 1946, the townspeople of Gainesville were aflutter with nervous excitement. Farm wives, merchants, and university students mingled beneath the oak and magnolia trees on the courthouse grounds. The more eager court-watchers were already seated in the balcony-lined courtroom of the old courthouse, the red brick heart of this thriving community of 20,000 citizens. When the clock in the courthouse steeple announced that 9:00 had arrived, the fortunate few who managed to find seats among the journalists, photographers, and lawyers breathlessly awaited the entrance of Judge John A. H. Murphree into the hot and crowded courtroom. They were expecting a spectacle to rival the greatest show on earth.

When it was all over, the participants in the *Cross Creek* trial spared no adjectives in describing it. To Phil May it was "interesting and dramatic ... the goddamnedest law suit that I ever even heard about." Kate Walton likened it to "a Roman circus." For Marjorie the trial was both "utterly vicious" and "hilariously funny." To one of the courtroom spectators, "it was as good as any show you ever went to in the world."

All in all, it was Gainesville's shining hour—the day the pages of *Cross Creek* came to life before a fascinated public. The fact that this was happening in a weighty lawsuit did little to dim the general exuberance for the event. The *Miami Herald* reported the opening of the trial with the zeal of a carnival barker:

"Cross Creek," with its original real-life cast—definitely not a motion picture—moves into this city Monday for an indefinite run in the circuit court room here.... Just about every other figure mentioned in the book except Dora, the Jersey cow, has been called as a witness.

As the trial wore on and filled the newspapers with scintillating gossip, increasing numbers of spectators descended on the crowded courtroom. So altogether entertaining was the unfolding drama that the lucky few with ringside seats were loath to give them up. A number of prominent Gainesville women saw the trial through from start to finish, having their lunches brought to them in the courtroom so that they could guard their spots.

Those outside the courtroom were treated to a mini-spectacle as the famous and homespun paraded into the legal arena amid flashbulbs and reporters. Even the entrance of the lawyers was dramatic. J. V. Walton arrived wearing an English safari helmet. He was accompanied by his daughter Kate, who was nearly the same height as her diminutive father. "Her general appearance was mannish, her countenance, resolute," one eyewitness recalled.

True to her quest for privacy, Zelma Cason entered the courthouse with a large bag held up to her face. The bag served two purposes. It shielded Zelma (whom the newspapers described as tiny, gray-haired, and wearing wire-rimmed glasses) from the dreaded photographers and the prying eyes of the curious. It also contained knitting needles and yarn, which Zelma transformed into a blue sweater as the trial progressed. Norton Baskin sat near her at the large table reserved for lawyers and litigants in front of Judge Murphree's bench. As Zelma knitted, her ball of yarn—through intent or accident—repeatedly fell from her lap and rolled under the table.

Baskin, being the gentleman that he was, stooped down
each time to retrieve it.

Marjorie's entrances were always conspicuous despite
an early effort to maintain a conservative image. The
Gainesville Daily Sun reported that on the first day of the
trial Marjorie was solemnly attired: "Miss Rawlings
wore a severely plain brown dress, plain white beads,
and a little spot of a hat low over the right eye." Marjorie's later appearances were not so disappointing to the
fashion-conscious. She arrived other days wearing more
flamboyant headgear, on one occasion motoring in from
Cross Creek in an open-topped jeep with her hand
grasping a wide-brimmed hat. She was heard to remark
upon alighting from the jeep: "Now I know how Marie
Antoinette felt on the tumbrel!"

The news media followed the women's fashions as
closely as the trial testimony. On the third day of trial the
Tampa Morning Tribune reported:

> Mrs. Rawlings appeared wearing the same pastel
> sport frock she wore yesterday but minus the
> panama hat. Miss Cason, sitting on the opposite side
> of the table occupied by the principals and their
> lawyers, changed from yesterday's polka dot to a
> navy blue number, with a fresh gardenia. . . . Miss
> Cason was wearing bright paint on her fingernails.
> Mrs. Rawlings none.

But more serious matters than the color of their finger-
nails awaited the litigants inside the courtroom. On the
bench, Judge John Murphree had gaveled the courtroom
to order.

Judge Murphree—by history and judicial temperament—was a fitting choice to man the gavel in this
extraordinary lawsuit. Murphree was born in Tallahassee, the son of A. A. (Albert) Murphree, the second pres-

The trial

ident of the University of Florida. As an undergraduate at the University of Florida, the young Murphree played football and was president of his fraternity. After graduation from law school in 1928 he practiced law in Gainesville and served a term in the Florida legislature. Murphree was defeated in a race for county judge, a loss he soon came to view as fortuitous when he was appointed to the higher circuit judgeship. He served on the Alachua County Circuit Court for thirty-five years, until his retirement in 1978.

During the *Cross Creek* trial the youthful Murphree weathered the storms of hilarity that often rocked his Gainesville courtroom with a happy combination of southern gentility, humor, and common sense. He had an easygoing manner that did not unduly dampen the spirited atmosphere of the proceedings, a trait that one newspaper heralded in its report of the trial:

> In his early 40's, a bespectacled and naturally a cheerful fellow, [Judge Murphree is] having a tough time maintaining the judicial calm when the testimony gets really hilarious, as it frequently does. . . . [H]e once hid his face behind a handkerchief to conceal his laughter.

Judge Murphree's role was to rule on motions and objections, while the ultimate question of the defendants' liability was in the hands of the jury. But Judge Murphree followed the trial testimony with the same riveted attention as the jurors, making trial notes and (as was his custom) pencil sketches of the witnesses to aid his memory. With the practiced eye of an artist, he later told his family that Zelma Cason did, indeed, resemble the "angry and efficient canary" of Marjorie's description. Judge Murphree's real contribution to the trial was his sense of fairness and decorum; his judicial personality was best summed up by Marjorie herself—who pronounced him "a swell person." After the trial, Marjorie remembered him each year at Christmas with a gift of oranges from her grove.

The first order of business was the selection of a six-man jury—six men because the jury list was exclusively male. Not until 1949 did Florida change its laws to permit women to serve on juries. Even then women were assigned special female bailiffs, ordered to use separate lodging and bathroom facilities, and prohibited from hearing eminent domain cases.

The list of fifty prospective jurors was eventually whittled down to six jurors and two alternates. Many jurors (including several who claimed they were about to leave town) were excused by the judge from active service. Others were struck from the panel by the parties' lawyers in an effort to arrive at an impartial jury. Among the questions asked the prospective jurors during the voir dire was whether they had read the book *Cross Creek*. Much to Marjorie's amusement, none of them had.

Sigsbee Scruggs was in charge of jury selection for the defense team, and he did his job admirably. He successfully excluded from the panel two prospective jurors who believed that an author should obtain consent from living characters mentioned in a book. All the jurors chosen were young crackers, inclined by geography and sentiment to sympathize with Marjorie. And one of the jurors, J. H. White, seemed frankly favorable to the defense. When asked during the voir dire if he objected to the use of real names in biography, he responded: "I don't; because if I did, and everybody else did, there would be no history books written." A local newspaper opined: "The spectators don't know yet why the plaintiff accepted him."

The six jurors selected were Harold Coles, foreman, a Gainesville jeweler; Allison Folds, proprietor of a Gainesville hardware store; Edgar S. Dunn, a Gainesville candy dealer; Harry M. Baker, operator of a Hawthorne turpentine business; E. D. Hartman, a Gainesville carpenter; and J. H. White, an automobile electrical worker fresh from the armed forces. Two alternate jurors were selected: G. W. Brabham, Sr., and M. J. Hunter, both farmers. Phil May had investigated each juror's background before the trial to prepare for jury selection. His strategy was to pick a panel "of literate men, free from prejudice and who enjoy some economic security." The six jurors seemed to fit this mold.

The jury selection took most of Monday, and the lawyers agreed to call one witness out of order late that day. He was Leland Hiatt, state welfare commissioner of Florida, who was subpoenaed by the defense. Mr. Hiatt had brought Zelma's personnel file, and he testified briefly about her duties as district welfare visitor. At the end of this testimony, Judge Murphree rapped the gavel to close the first day's proceedings.

Day Two of the *Cross Creek* trial began at 9:30 Tuesday morning with the swearing-in en masse of the remaining witnesses. Zelma had thirteen witnesses sworn, of whom six (including Zelma and her brother) testified. Marjorie had fifty-five witnesses sworn, of whom twenty-six testified. She also introduced into evidence the depositions of six defense witnesses who were unable to attend the trial, bringing to thirty-two the number of witnesses testifying on her behalf.

Zelma's counsel threw a temporary scare into the defendants by including Norton Baskin among the prospective witnesses (apparently intending to use his testimony to establish Marjorie's financial worth), and then invoking a court rule requiring all witnesses to remove themselves from the courtroom when not testifying. Phil May rose to the occasion by pointing out that Baskin was himself being sued for $100,000, as spouse of the famous author. The judge agreed that he should be permitted to remain in the courtroom. Though Baskin was never actually called as a witness, Marjorie couldn't resist teasing him. "You think we ought to take him to lunch with us?" she asked May playfully. "He's going over to the other side."

After the witnesses were sworn, J. V. Walton and Sigsbee Scruggs made brief opening remarks to the jury. Walton then opened the plaintiff's case by calling Zelma Cason as his first witness. Zelma laid down her knitting and marched determinedly to the witness stand. She would remain there all of Tuesday and much of Wednesday.

Under questioning by her lawyer, Zelma described her life in short, almost terse phrases. She was born (she falsely testified) in 1893. Her girlhood in Island Grove was ordinary and uneventful. She had never engaged in business or earned a salary until her census-taking activities in 1930. She had since led a quiet life as a visitor with the State Welfare Board. She shunned publicity and notoriety of any kind.

Zelma then described her first meeting with Marjorie in Jacksonville, their "intimate friendship" and ultimate rift. She did not consent to be a character in *Cross Creek*, she declared, and she didn't know that Marjorie had written about her until she was teased about it at the office. Among the consequences of her public humiliation was that she now avoided using the name "Zelma" when answering the telephone, and she no longer went out to eat. In addition, the distress had caused a flare-up of her "ulcerated stomach," and she had been required to follow a strict diet for several months.

Zelma displayed some of her famous feistiness when Walton questioned her about specific passages from *Cross Creek*:

Q: It then says: "Zelma is an ageless spinster resembling an angry and efficient canary.". . . Do you know in what respect you resembled an angry and efficient canary?

A: I would not know.

Q: Did that reference please you?

A: It did not. I don't think I have ever seen an angry canary, or an efficient one either, and my mother raised them. . . .

Q: It next says: "I cannot decide whether she should have been a man or a mother." How did you take that reference?

A: I resented it. I didn't like it at all. I have no resemblance, I don't think, of a man. . . .

Q: It says next: "She combines the more violent characteristics of both. . . ." Have you violent characteristics, to your knowledge?

A: Not that I know of. . . .

Q: Now [a story involving Marjorie's horse bolting and the resulting wild ride] concludes with this: "But all I had from Zelma was her special brand of profanity for having lost the sweet potatoes." Did you use any profanity on her having lost any sweet potatoes?

A: I have never used the Lord's name in vain in my life.

Phil May's cross-examination of Zelma occupied the rest of Day Two. Zelma was a curt and reticent witness under May's probing questions, often claiming an inability to recall a date or circumstance.

Zelma admitted under cross-examination that she had once been released from her employment at the Gainesville office of the State Welfare Board and was later transferred to Palatka. She denied that her legendary temper was the cause for her dismissal, but when pressed she could not give another reason. She reluctantly conceded a proclivity toward political activism, confessing only: "I have asked my friends to vote for people that are friends of mine." She also admitted taking part in a school board meeting concerning the dismissal of an Island Grove teacher, while insisting that she couldn't remember her own role in the controversy.

May was encouraged by Zelma's stubbornness and believed she was losing credibility with her frequent claim "I don't recall." He decided to challenge her testimony that she never used profanity:

Q: Are you accustomed to using strong expressions to emphasize statements?

A: What do you mean by that?

Q: I think the question is sufficiently clear for an answer.

A: Not unless I was angry.

Q: Do you have a fairly high temper?

A: I would not say that I do.

Q: You do have outbursts of temper on occasions when you are outraged; do you not?

A: I do not.

Q: Then you do not have a high temper?

A: I don't consider I do.

Q: Have you ever used the term, "bastard" in your conversation?

A: I have.

Q: Have you ever used the word, "son-of-a-bitch" in your conversation?

A: I have.

Q: Have you used those terms to emphasize statements that you would be making?

A: I would not answer that. I don't know.

Q: Have you ever directed those terms at particular individuals?

A: One.

Q: Only one?

A: I recall one. . . .

Q: Would you swear that there were not any more than the one?

A: I could not.

With this high and unholy drama the court recessed for the day. It reconvened at 9:30 A.M. on Wednesday, Day Three. Before returning to Zelma's testimony, Judge Murphree sought to allay the jurors' fears (apparently occasioned by some misleading newspaper reports) that a finding of punitive damages in the case might carry a criminal penalty—even a jail term—for Florida's most famous authoress. If the jury found that Marjorie acted with malice, the judge declared, then it could award punitive as well as actual damages to Zelma. But this was a civil case, so there would be no criminal penalty. At Walton's request, Judge Murphree also agreed to instruct the jurors (who were not sequestered at night) to refrain from reading the newspaper accounts that were now flooding the community.

Zelma was then recalled to the witness stand for further cross-examination. May offered into evidence portions of Zelma's employment records and used them to challenge her earlier testimony that she had not been gainfully employed before 1930. She had, in fact, been employed for brief periods during World War I and had helped to manage her brother's orange grove. May also scored some points on the question of damages. Zelma admitted that she'd had an ulcerated stomach since 1926, often aggravated by her problems at work. Her weight was now 120 pounds, up from her pre–*Cross Creek* weight of 108. But Zelma insisted that the book had caused her condition to deteriorate. Only today, she announced, she had taken medication to sustain herself during the trial. "I have it right here in my pocketbook," she assured May.

The lawyers completed their questioning shortly before noon, and Zelma stepped down from the witness box. But to everyone's surprise she paused, turned, and returned to the stand. She began to seat herself again. "Mr. May," she said, "I want to say one thing —." Whereupon Walton touched her arm and implored:

"Come down, please; come down. That does not matter." Zelma obediently quitted the witness box without, after all, having had the last word.

Walton then called his next witness. Bert Ergle was the stepfather of Harry Barnes, the young man who had been identified by name in "Cracker Chidlings." Ergle's testimony was intended to show the grief this had caused Barnes's mother, thus supporting Zelma's claim that Marjorie had acted with malice. But Judge Murphree sustained defense objections to the testimony, declaring: "[W]e can't try every character in all of these books."

Walton was now forced to abandon his plan to use Mrs. Ergle as a witness. He decided to call three more witnesses: Mary Carn, Alice M. Ellis, and Mrs. J. Edward Preston. Walton asked the court: "If your Honor please, we are going to call some ladies and is it permissible for my daughter to conduct their examination?" The court's permission having been obtained, Kate Walton at last took her place before the bar.

Under Kate's questioning, Mary Carn testified that she was an employee of the State Welfare Board in St. Augustine who had known Zelma "for years and years and years." Zelma, she declared, was just an ordinary human being without the violent characteristics ascribed to her in *Cross Creek:*

Q: [I]s Miss Cason a blasphemous woman?
A: I would not think so.
Q: Is she profane?
A: No.
Q: Does she take the Lord's name in vain?
A: No, I never heard that.

On cross-examination, Sigsbee Scruggs sought to undermine Miss Carn's testimony by showing that Zelma had helped her to secure her present job. He then turned to the ever-popular question of Zelma's profanity:

Q: You stated, Miss Carn, that you had never heard her use the Lord's name in vain. You understand what is meant by ordinary cussing?

A: Yes.

Q: Have you ever heard her use those types of words?

A: I think I have. . . .

Q: During the period of time that you have been with her, have you heard her use the epithet, "bastard"?

A: No, I never have.

Q: Have you heard her use the epithet, "son-of-a-bitch"?

A: I don't think so.

Q: Have you ever heard her use the word, "damn"?

A: I have heard her use that quite often.

Alice M. Ellis, a social worker, was called to the witness stand. Mrs. Ellis testified that Zelma was not officious, bad-tempered, or mannishly violent, though she did have an inclination to nervousness. Moreover, declared the witness, "I have never heard her use profanity." On cross-examination, Mrs. Ellis admitted that Zelma was firm and forceful in her opinions, but insisted that she was "essentially feminine." The Zelma of Alice Ellis's memory was decidedly not the Zelma of Marjorie's pen.

Mrs. J. Edward Preston, housewife, was the last witness to be called by Kate Walton. Zelma had lived with Mrs. Preston for two years in Palatka while she was stationed there as a welfare worker. Mrs. Preston testified that Zelma was deeply hurt and troubled by the book, thus aggravating her ulcerated stomach. Zelma, she declared, was mild-mannered, sensitive, and compassionate. She had never seen her angry, never heard her use profanity. Marjorie's portrayal of Zelma in *Cross Creek* was "definitely the opposite of the Miss Cason I had become so intimately acquainted with." With this laudatory and ladylike description of their client, the Waltons rested their case.

On Wednesday afternoon the defense opened their case, and the assault on Zelma's claim to delicacy began. The first witness was Noel Moore, deputy sheriff of Island Grove for twenty-eight years. Mr. Moore hadn't read *Cross Creek*, but he did have decided opinions on the character of Zelma Cason. Zelma, he asserted, was an active partisan in local political races, and she had tried to influence the school board against hiring a certain teacher. Under questioning by Sigsbee Scruggs, Moore described Zelma's reputation in the community:

Q: You say you have known Miss Cason for a considerable period of time. Just state to the jury what kind of personage she is insofar as her temperament and manner of speech and so forth is concerned.

A: Well, she is a person who takes part in anything most comes up in the community, one side and the other, and just tries to ruin or rule.

Q: Have you ever heard her express herself concerning various matters?

A: Why, quite a bit, yes.

Q: What kind of language does she ordinarily use?

A: She uses profanity, usually; "damn," "bastard," or "son-of-a-bitch."

Q: Have you heard that yourself?

A: I have.

During cross-examination by J. V. Walton, the reason

for Moore's first-hand knowledge of Zelma's profanity became abundantly clear:

Q: You stated that—you said that you heard her call somebody a son-of-a-bitch; was that person you?
A: Yes.
Q: You were the one she called a son-of-a-bitch?
A: Yes, I am the son-of-a-bitch.

The spectators in the crowded courtroom—some of them wedged in the windowsills—roared with laughter. Zelma Cason looked up from her knitting and smiled.

There followed a two-day procession of witnesses who amused and enlightened the jury with stories of Zelma's disposition. Many testified that any person of "ordinary sensibilities" would be unoffended, even flattered, by Marjorie's caricature. Mrs. Chase Maddox, Jr., of Alachua County testified that she considered the pen-sketch of Zelma entirely inoffensive. The sedate Mrs. Maddox proved to be a durable witness, whom even the insistent cross-examination of Kate Walton could not budge:

Q: Mrs. Maddox, would you mind if three hundred thousand people thought you were profane and blasphemous and habitually took the name of the Lord in vain? . . .
A: If I talked that way, I would not mind anyone knowing that I did.

The elderly Mrs. J. W. McCollum of Gainesville, who described Zelma as "a very charmingly outspoken person," also found Marjorie's description inoffensive. "[T]he portrayal . . . was delightful," she assured the jury. Several witnesses were called to testify that they —unlike the hypersensitive Miss Cason—had no objection to being mentioned in *Cross Creek*. Dessie Smith testified that she wasn't at all offended by Marjorie's reference to her salty language in the chapter "Hyacinth Drift." Nor was neighbor Tom Glisson offended by his or Zelma's portrayal: "[K]nowing Miss Cason ... I figured it was a pretty good description of her, maybe with a lot of truth; the same as what she wrote about me, maybe there was a lot of truth in that." Thelma Shortridge, daughter of the late Fred Tompkins, told the jury she loved her father's treatment in the book: "[I]t was of him truly." Moreover, no true Cross Creekian would be the least insulted by reference to his or her salty language: "[I]f you don't use a few [of those words] you can't stay there!" she exclaimed. The courtroom exploded in laughter, as Judge Murphree rapped helplessly for order.

Zelma's profanity was exposed in scintillating detail. Mrs. Freddie Lee Whitlock, proprietor of a wholesale fish and boat rental business in Cross Creek, recounted with an air of offended propriety her first meeting with Zelma:

> I was at the house ... for some business, and went back to the creek ... and when I got back to the creek I noticed I had new business.... I heard a lady say, "Here's the woman I want to see." Well, never seeing the woman before in my life, naturally I asked her what I could do, and she said she wanted a "God damn paddle with a nail in it." It kind of hit me, her talking like that. She said, "I want to catch me some God damn fish."

Carey Dyess, proprietor of the "juke joint" on Zelma's Island Grove rental property, testified that he frequently heard Zelma utter such invectives as "[d]amn, God damn, son-of-a-bitch and bastard, and such as that." A director of the District Welfare Board testified that Zelma had embarrassed him by commenting to his subordinates: "Hell! I used to change his diapers."

Other defense witnesses told the jury about Zelma's meddling in civic affairs. A resident of nearby Lochloosa testified that Zelma had cornered him and criticized Deputy Sheriff Noel Moore. A former candidate for Alachua County tax collector recounted how Zelma threatened she would use her influence against his election. The candidate was defeated. A member of the Alachua County Board of Public Instruction testified that Zelma had spoken at a 1940 board meeting against the retention of a school teacher, accusing the teacher's proponents of forging signatures on a petition.

Zelma's lawyers had had enough. This testimony was definitely hurting their client's image in the minds of the jurors. J. V. Walton asked the court to exclude further evidence of this nature, arguing that the truth of Marjorie's description of Zelma was not an issue in the case. Scruggs remonstrated that Marjorie intended to call five more witnesses who were characters out of *Cross Creek* and three more witnesses to testify to "the strong and forceful language of Miss Cason." Judge Murphree, himself probably wearied by the parade of witnesses spouting four-letter words, responded that such testimony would be cumulative. Scruggs did not call his additional witnesses.

But the defense wasn't through yet. Other witnesses were called to support a somewhat loftier defense strategy. May believed that if he could prove *Cross Creek* was vital to the public interest, the book would be immune from Zelma's mean-spirited attack. So interspersed with the folksier witnesses were men of letters, whose testimony was intended to impress the jurors with the public prominence of Marjorie's writings.

The first literary witness was Dr. Alfred J. Hanna, professor of history at Rollins College. May began the direct examination of Dr. Hanna with an inquiry about his real qualifications to testify:

Q: Do you regard yourself as a Florida "cracker"?
A: I do.
Q: Are you proud of it?
A: I am very proud of it.

Having impressed the cracker jury with this salient fact, May asked Dr. Hanna to testify about the importance of Marjorie's work.

Cross Creek, Dr. Hanna declared, was a book of "rare simplicity." It was even more valuable to Florida than *The Yearling,* because it "offset the gaudy 'honky-tonk' of the tourist publicity" and gave a "clear, keen picture" of life in the state. Marjorie Kinnan Rawlings was undoubtedly the most prominent writer in Florida. She was also the recipient of three honorary degrees from Florida colleges and universities, the only woman to be so honored.

May summoned another scholarly witness to bolster this laudatory testimony. Dr. Clifford P. Lyons, professor of English literature at the University of Florida, compared Marjorie's writings to those of Mark Twain. He noted that *Cross Creek* had been greeted with "almost one continuous chorus of praise" from critics throughout the United States. From a literary standpoint, the portrayal of Zelma was nothing less than splendid, even patriotic:

It is a representation of a type of person which is very much admired in America; self reliant, able to take care of one's self in any circumstances, even under conditions which approach hardships. It has something in it of the pioneer kind of thing. . . . It is a great tradition in American literature; as democratic as the country.

Sandwiched between these ebullient voices of professorial praise was the testimony of Lt. Bertram C. Cooper, a handsome, six-foot Navy chaplain. Lieutenant Cooper's presence in the courtroom was a happy accident for the defense. He and Marjorie had become friends through his admiring fan letters. He had heard about the trial, found his way to the courthouse, and greeted Marjorie enthusiastically the day before. Norton Baskin recalled the noisy scene:

> He came flying up there and he came in at a recess. And half-way down [the courtroom aisle] he shouted to Marjorie, "What are these bastards trying to do to you?" And they embraced like hell and then he turned and said, "This has got to be Norton." So he picks me up!

Lieutenant Cooper's appearance seemed so propitious that May decided to use him as a witness. J. V. Walton objected that Lieutenant Cooper had been present in the courtroom during other witnesses' testimony, but Judge Murphree overruled the objection. The witness was sworn in before the jury, an imposing figure in his naval uniform and chaplain's cross.

Lieutenant Cooper testified that *Cross Creek* was an emotional lifesaver for the servicemen on the U.S.S. *Bountiful,* a hospital ship. He had passed out copies of the armed forces edition as tonic for the homesick men, and the book "was like a long letter from home." The men particularly liked Marjorie's mouth-watering chapter on food, "Our Daily Bread." The audience roared with laughter.

On cross-examination, J. V. Walton tried to show that Lieutenant Cooper was a biased witness. "Didn't I see you and Mrs. Baskin embrace very affectionately when you met in the courtroom yesterday?" he asked. Lieutenant Cooper responded that because of Marjorie's kindness in sending him books for his men, he was "quite enthusiastically glad to see her." And being from

Savannah, "it would be most unnatural for me to walk up to a good friend of mine and shake hands with them." Walton, seeing the futility of his position, declined further cross-examination.

May excited the jury's sympathy with the testimony of yet another serviceman, despite the vigorous protests of Zelma's counsel. The deposition of James R. Peters, taken in Michigan before the trial, was admitted and read into evidence. Peters had served on several naval ships in the Pacific arena during World War II, including the ill-fated *Lexington*. When the *Lexington* was sunk by enemy fire on May 7, 1942, Peters raced to his locker and tucked his copy of *Cross Creek* into his lifejacket. The reason? Because *Cross Creek* was "one of the very best books that I have read," the serviceman declared.

Zelma's lawyers found it difficult to counter these literary and emotional tributes to the book, so they decided upon an unorthodox plan of attack. They would muzzle the voices of praise by showing that *Cross Creek* was actually vulgar and lascivious. In some of the most impassioned cross-examination of the trial, J. V. Walton and his co-counsel, E. A. Clayton, hammered the witnesses with questions about Marjorie's earthy, humorous writing style. It was a risky tactic, designed to shock the conscience of the cracker jury. It succeeded in enlivening the eager spectators, whom Judge Murphree had to repeatedly gavel to order.

It began with Walton's cross-examination of Dr. Alfred J. Hanna. "Would you not regard [*Cross Creek*] as a book rather unnecessarily interspersed with indelicacies and indecency and vulgarity and sexuality?" he asked. Dr. Hanna replied with offended dignity: "No, I would not, Sir." Walton now had the undivided attention of every person in the courtroom. He picked up a copy of *Cross Creek* and read aloud a passage in which Marjorie described her "shingle-butted" maid, Adrenna. Why, he queried, would such a thing be included in a purported autobiography? Dr. Hanna, not one to be outwitted, retorted that "the gentleman here is endeavoring to cast a slur on the situation by taking pieces out quite unwisely in relation to the whole."

Walton, book still in hand, read on:

> Q: ... I will read what it next says: "She [Adrenna] could seduce any man she wanted, for the moment, but she could not hold them, or, if they were faithful, she grew tired of them." Now, what is elegant, or informative of the author's life, or what part has that in an autobiography?

Dr. Hanna ignored Walton and turned to Judge Murphree: "Your Honor, is it necessary that a witness be harassed such as this?" To which Walton rejoined: "I don't know whether he thinks he is so eminent that he does not have to answer." Dr. Hanna, angry but still eminent, responded: "The passage, in my judgment, would contribute to the truth of life."

Walton then turned to another passage in *Cross Creek* where Marjorie described the incontinence of several puppies left alone on her front porch. "What is elegant about that passage?" Walton queried. "Isn't it a fact, Doctor, that passages like that are put in a book to appeal to the morbid, or semi-morbid?" The jury, in rapt attention, would never hear the answer. Phil May objected to the "hypothetical question," and Judge Murphree, who had heard quite enough, sustained the objection. Dr. Hanna stepped down from the witness stand and, in a display of southern gentility, shook hands with Walton as he left the courtroom.

May believed that the cross-examination had piqued the jury's interest, and he decided to capitalize on this appeal to the "morbid." He offered into evidence six copies of the book, so that each juror could come to his own conclusion about its alleged vulgarity. Walton objected that a single, autographed copy of the book was already in evidence. But Judge Murphree, recognizing that Walton himself had opened this Pandora's box, overruled the objection. No one doubted what the members of the jury would be reading that night. After the verdict each juror would ask Marjorie to autograph his copy of *Cross Creek* as a remembrance of the trial.

Undaunted, Zelma's counsel continued their efforts to undermine the book's credibility. Walton's associate counsel, E. A. Clayton, cross-examined Dr. Clifford P. Lyons. Clayton pointed to Marjorie's description of the breeding of hogs, and he asked the witness if this was his idea of "good literature." Dr. Lyons conceded that the passage was "salty, and racy," but he nevertheless insisted that it was, indeed, good literature.

Clayton then turned to a passage where Marjorie described a favorite old outhouse, on whose walls hung a French sonnet. Was this not lewd and inelegant? I can't answer that, Dr. Lyons responded, because "I don't know what the verse said." The spectators burst into uncontrolled laughter. Judge Murphree threatened to clear the courtroom if the general merriment did not cease. The crowd, subdued, heard the witness have the last word on the subject. Even the Bible, he declared, at times contained passages "which could, in no stretch of our imagination be called delicate or elegant." Not daring to take on the Bible as well as *Cross Creek*, Clayton ended his cross-examination.

On Friday morning, Day Five, the defense finished questioning the last of its supporting witnesses. The moment that everyone was waiting for had arrived. Spectators were three-deep in the balcony and crowded the halls outside the courtroom. The crush of onlookers (including, as one newspaper reported, "the attractive wife of Judge John A. H. Murphree") leaned forward expectantly. The press sat with pencils poised. At about 10:00,

Phil May turned to his star witness. "The defense calls Marjorie Kinnan Rawlings," he announced.

Marjorie rose from the counsel table and took her place in the witness box. She would remain there the rest of Friday and all day Monday. Her two-day testimony, occupying nearly a hundred pages of the trial record, would constitute one of the most important historical records of her life and writings. But the courtroom audience was not expecting such a lofty by-product of Marjorie's testimony. They were expecting to be amused and amazed by her performance. They would not be disappointed.

Chapter Seven

The Jury Returns

Marjorie Kinnan Rawlings was more than just a local celebrity to those who awaited her trial testimony. She was, they knew, a world-famous author and a colleague of the literary greats. She was also an earthy, friendly, and funny woman. It was obvious that Zelma was swimming against a sympathetic current running strongly in favor of her opponent. Those in the courtroom—including the jury—were ready to hear what Marjorie had to say in her own defense. They were also ready to believe her and love her. She won them over completely.

Overcoming a tendency toward intense shyness (a trait that only those closest to her glimpsed), Marjorie summoned her courage and was "cool as a cucumber" in her two days of testimony. One newspaper described her as "an uninhibited and unorthodox witness" who "threw the courtroom into an uproar" with her wit. Marjorie's lawyers had drilled her extensively on the facts of the case and proper courtroom decorum. But it was her frankness and humor that captivated judge, jurors, press, and spectators alike. Indeed, the only person who seemed unmoved by her testimony was Zelma Cason, who, the press reported, "sat and knitted with only an occasional glance toward the witness stand as Mrs. Rawlings offered her defense."

Phil May began his direct examination by asking Marjorie to identify two photographs of her home at Cross Creek. These photos were then introduced into evidence, despite Walton's objection that they were irrelevant to the case. May continued his questioning: "Do you have a profession?" "I have two professions," Marjorie affirmed. "Perhaps one is a profession and one is a business. By profession, I am a writer." "What is your business?" asked May. "An orange grower," the witness replied.

May then asked a series of questions concerning Marjorie's youth, marriage to Charles Rawlings, and early career as a writer. Marjorie described the young couple's move to Florida in 1928, their difficult years on the grove, their divorce, and her decision "to stay there alone and fight it out." Marjorie had to contend with more than just the frost and dismal crops; the real struggle was with her sense of failure as a writer. One newspaper reported that she "verged briefly on tears" as she told the packed courtroom:

> I was in great despair about my writings. I had been trying to do so-called "popular" writings . . . and they just were not any good; and when I came to Florida and was so enchanted with the country and the people, I put all thought of writing from a popular angle for a woman's magazine and that sort of thing behind me, and I decided to go at this new material in an entirely different way. . . . Instead of presenting plot and drama, I was interpreting this lovely country and these people as they appealed to me; and I decided that if that sort of writing was not wanted, wasn't acceptable, I would not try to write any more.

May turned to the subject of Marjorie's friendship with Zelma. Marjorie explained that she and Zelma had been close friends since her own first days at the Creek, and that Zelma had encouraged her efforts to write about Florida. May handed Marjorie a copy of *Cross Creek*, opened to the description of Zelma, and asked her to "interpret it as it was written in your mind and heart."

Marjorie's testimony revealed as much of the writer as the subject:

> I had to sit down and think, now how do you describe Zelma? What is she? She is not a married woman. I could not describe her as an old maid, because I think of an old maid as a woman who is not married because she has not had an opportunity. Zelma had always had admiration from men and opportunities to marry. So I thought "spinster" was the only term. . . . And Zelma's age didn't enter into it in my mind. I thought, "How does she look?" Ever since I had known her she hadn't changed much in appearance. She was a woman who didn't grow old. I think it answers the description exactly, "ageless spinster."
>
> "Resembling an angry and efficient canary." Mother Rawlings was always very fond of Zelma and Zelma's hair was very golden and she has blue eyes, and she was small and quick, and Mother used to call her, "Blue and gold." . . . So "resembling an angry and efficient canary." Angry, yes, on occasions, and efficient at all times. . . .
>
> "I cannot decide whether she should have been a man or a mother." In my mind there was no thought of describing her as mannish. By that I simply meant that her abilities were more or less wasted. If she had been a man she would have been an executive; she might have gone into law; might have been a doctor; but she had great talents and great ability that a man could have done more with. ". . . should have been a man or a mother." I have never known anyone who loved children as much as she, or cares more for any children, black and white.

Marjorie testified that she had taken some precautions in writing about other people in Cross Creek, but it had never occurred to her that Zelma might be hurt or offended:

> Zelma knew that I was a writer; knew that I used whatever material seemed to me interesting and artistic for my purpose within my limitations; had helped me with material; and perhaps more for this than any other reason, that she had been so partisan in smoothing things over when I had inadvertently offended Harry Barnes' mother. She was so helpful and partisan about that, that I could not conceive of her being offended in herself.

May closed his direct examination with some questions concerning Marjorie's finances between 1918 and 1938. He hoped to refute the charge that Marjorie profited mightily at Zelma's expense by showing there had been many lean years at the Creek. Marjorie testified that she and Charles Rawlings had fairly good incomes from their newspaper work before coming to Florida in 1928. The years from 1928 to 1935, however, were "desperate." From 1935 to 1938 her finances "eased considerably," but she was not financially secure until publication of *The Yearling* in 1938. With this modest appraisal of his client's financial worth, May closed his direct examination.

It was nearly noon on Friday when May ended his questioning, and Judge Murphree recessed for lunch until 2:00 P.M. Marjorie's testimony had been articulate, at times moving, but not otherwise spectacular. After lunch J. V. Walton would change that rather sedate state of affairs. His cross-examination would be lengthy and provocative, goading Marjorie to a full display of her famous wit. Their often hilarious exchanges were the highlight of the trial for the rapt gallery of spectators and press.

Walton skipped from one topic to another during his

questioning, a favorite trick of cross-examiners who hope to catch their subject off-guard. Marjorie was equal to the challenge. Walton began by asking her where her home was. "I never had a home elsewhere than Cross Creek," Marjorie replied. Then why, Walton asked, did you challenge the venue of this lawsuit by claiming you lived in St. Augustine? Marjorie finessed the answer with the skill of a lawyer: "As long, I presume . . . as I am with my husband in his legal residence, which is St. Augustine, I am a resident with him of wherever he is."

Walton turned to more solid ground. He questioned Marjorie at length about her relationship with Zelma. Marjorie's answers were direct, detailed, and articulate. Walton handed the witness a copy of *Cross Creek* and led her through a word-for-word apologia of her description of Zelma. Marjorie did not budge from the answers she had given in May's direct examination.

Marjorie's candor was unnerving and permitted little leeway for an attack on her credibility as a witness. Walton quoted a passage from *Cross Creek* in which Marjorie had written: "One man's meat is another man's poison more certainly in literature than in gastronomy." Did you realize when you wrote the book that it might be meat to one and poison to another? Walton asked. "Surely." "You realized that?" "Oh, yes." Can you understand, Walton continued, why a person might not want to be published in a book such as this? "Not the average person," Marjorie responded. "My experience has not been that the average person objected at all; usually, very much the contrary."

Marjorie was proving a tough nut to crack. Walton began asking more provocative questions. Marjorie's answers became more insistent and clever. What did you mean, Walton asked, by referring to Zelma's "special brand of profanity"? Zelma's cussing, Marjorie explained, "is a little different from my cussing, or Thelma Shortridge's cussing. It is a matter of style." Was the

phrase "my profane friend Zelma" intended to mean
that Zelma was blasphemous? "Not in the way I understand blasphemous, no. Just common country cussing."
Did Marjorie ever indulge in a little profanity herself?
"Oh, yes." "Quite frequently?" "Oh, yes.... I think
Zelma and I would about have to divide honors for our
reputation for cussing."

By now the courtroom audience was warming to its
subject. This was the kind of spirited crossfire they had
come hoping to hear. To their delight, Walton turned
next to the story in *Cross Creek* concerning the demise of
Mr. Martin's marauding pig. Did you enjoy shooting the
pig? Walton asked. "I did enjoy shooting it, yes." The
spectators were chuckling, and Judge Murphree tried to
suppress a smile. Walton continued,

> Q: Did you shoot that pig regardless of whether it
>   was illegal or not?
> A: I felt under the circumstances I had every right
>   to shoot it.
> Q: Though it was another's and though it might be
>   against the law?
> A: Though it was another's and might be against
>   the law?
> Q: Yes.
> A: Yes.

Walton was hoping to convince the jury that Marjorie
had no respect for the law. If she could shoot Mr.
Martin's pig without regret, she'd just as soon do the
same to Zelma. Marjorie wasn't about to be trapped.
"You are trying to draw an analogy by my shooting an
outlaw pig and by describing 'My friend Zelma' as profane, and I think that is dreadful," she accused Walton. "I
have a profound regard for law. My father was a lawyer
and he inculcated that in me."

Walton tried again. He turned to the story in *Cross*

Creek where Marjorie and her brother had returned from a deer hunt to find her house in ruins and the hired help full of moonshine. Marjorie and her brother had grabbed their guns and confronted the drunken offenders. Walton misread a portion of the story, and Marjorie corrected him. She then took the offensive. Didn't the law permit her to defend her own tenant house? Walton started to answer her question. May objected, "[T]his has gone too far." Walton retorted, "It is the witness' question he is objecting to." Judge Murphree, as puzzled as everyone else, added his voice to the confusion: "I think we have this backwards." By now, all order had vanished from the crowded courtroom. The *Miami Herald* reported:

> The case at hand was almost forgotten in the argument over this question. Judge Murphree hid his face behind his handkerchief to conceal his laughter. The audience didn't conceal theirs and the baliff [*sic*] rapped for order—without complete success.

Walton's cross-examination then took on what one newspaper described as "a rabelaisian flavor." Isn't *Cross Creek* "rather replete with indecencies?" he asked. "It was not my intention, certainly, to make it so." Still pressing, Walton continued: "It has more or less of vulgarity in it; has it not?" "I would call certain passages and certain incidents . . . vulgar, yes, but of the soil . . . part of the life, and so in the picture," Marjorie replied frankly. "Have you counted the lovely passages; passages that I think even you might not object to?"

By now Judge Murphree was growing impatient. He declared that the book was in evidence and could speak for itself. Walton was directed to proceed to another line of questioning. Further argument was prevented by the lateness of the hour. Marjorie was excused from the witness stand until Monday.

On Monday morning, Day Six, Walton resumed his cross-examination of Marjorie. He was determined to continue the assault on *Cross Creek*'s artistic merit. What about the outhouse story? And the stories about animal mating habits? Marjorie conceded amiably that the outhouse story was "distinctly vulgar" and "right down to earth." But the passages about the breeding of animals were another matter. It's all part of life in a rural community, she insisted, and the descriptions were clinically accurate. Indeed, *Time Magazine* had published several letters to the editor challenging and corroborating the accuracy of her sow-breeding story under the heading "She Knows Her Hogs." These things might be "common" or "earthy," Marjorie admitted, but they were "of legitimate interest in a rural book."

Walton continued his barrage of questions, determined now to portray *Cross Creek* as "cruel and hurtful." He had some real ammunition for this line of questioning—the scathing letter Marjorie had received in 1942 from an irate relative of George Fairbanks. Marjorie had humorously portrayed Fairbanks in *Cross Creek* as tongue-tied, more than a little fond of corn liquor, and often dependent on the good graces of his neighbors. Marjorie insisted that she had meant no harm and that Fairbanks had taken no offense at the story. But the letter accused Marjorie of insensitivity in publicizing Fairbanks's handicap and misfortunes. The letter further chastised Marjorie for making "marketable copy" out of stories about another Cross Creek resident, whom Marjorie had identified in the book as "my friend Moe."

Walton wished to offer this letter, and Marjorie's written reply, as exhibits in the case. Marjorie protested that the letter contained a reference to Moe's last name, something she had studiously avoided in her book. Could the letter be introduced without the name? "Which piece is it that you would like cut out?" Walton asked. Marjorie showed him, and he removed his pocket knife and cut out the offending word. The mutilated exhibit was offered into evidence.

As Walton neared the end of his cross-examination he began to probe Marjorie's financial condition, hoping to impress the modest jury with the famed author's wealth. "What is your net worth?" he asked. Phil May rose to object to the question. Judge Murphree overruled the objection, noting that May himself had opened up the subject by introducing photographs of Marjorie's home. May protested that the photos were intended only to show the simple life Marjorie led at Cross Creek, and he asked for a short adjournment to permit Marjorie to do a little figuring. Marjorie returned to the counsel table to do some quick computations on the back of an envelope.

While Marjorie was busy calculating her net worth, Walton asked Judge Murphree's permission to call a rebuttal witness out of the usual order. Zelma's brother, Dr. T. Z. Cason, was waiting patiently for his turn to testify, but he had to return to his medical practice in Jacksonville. The request was granted, and Dr. Cason took the stand for what turned out to be just a few minutes of testimony. Before he could answer several questions put to him by Walton, May objected that the testimony was not properly in rebuttal of evidence presented by the defense. Judge Murphree sustained most of May's objections, thwarting Walton's efforts to elicit testimony concerning Zelma's current physical condition, and leaving a gaping hole in Zelma's proof of damages. After a brief period of cross-examination Dr. Cason quit the witness stand, angry at his former friend Phil May and frustrated by his unproductive court appearance.

Marjorie resumed her testimony Monday afternoon. Walton again asked her to state her net worth. Marjorie answered that her net worth was approximately $124,000. Did she have any outstanding contracts to write other books or make movies? "I have no contracts of any sort at all," Marjorie responded. Satisfied, Walton closed his cross-examination.

But Phil May was not content to end his client's testimony with the jurors' minds filled with thoughts of filthy lucre. "Do you write for money?" he asked. "No." Why then, May continued, did she write? Marjorie replied:

Because it is in my blood and bones to write, you might say. I have done it so long. It is the thing I do, that's all; just as another man wants to be a carpenter, or something of the sort; and to interpret the Florida country that I love so, and the Florida people, to the best of my ability; and if it is received well and if it sells . . . it is simply good fortune.

And how would she describe her book, *Cross Creek*? May asked. If Marjorie hadn't already succeeded in winning the hearts of her listeners, she did so now with her answer:

To me, "Cross Creek" is a love story. It is a story of my love for the land, and for that particular portion of the land where I have felt that I belonged, which is Cross Creek. And when you love a person or a place, then their faults and peculiarities—that does not interfere with your love for them at all.

Determined to use his star witness to even greater advantage, May heightened his assault on the jury's sentiments. He asked Marjorie to read passages from *Cross Creek* that epitomized her feelings toward the Creek. Marjorie read humorous and moving passages from the book with the skill of a seasoned performer. Judge, jury, and spectators listened, enraptured. Zelma Cason steamed.

Marjorie reads from *Cross Creek* to the court

May ended his re-direct examination with an unsuccessful attempt to introduce thirty fan letters—a portion of hundreds of letters he had with him in the courtroom—to emphasize the public's enthusiasm for *Cross Creek*. Walton objected vigorously that these letters were irrelevant to the defense and constituted hearsay. Judge Murphree agreed, but May had already made his point to the jury. The *Miami Herald* reported:

> The fan letters were banned, but not before attorney May had paraded before the jury a couple of times with bulging envelopes of them, stacking them significantly on the desk of the court clerk. The lawyer spectators grinned widely and opinioned that if the May family raised any foolish children, Philip was not among them.

Marjorie was excused from further testimony, and May offered into evidence portions of several depositions of out-of-state witnesses taken before trial. In order to dramatize the testimony for the jury, May read the questions aloud and asked Sigsbee Scruggs to assume the witness stand and take the role of the deponents. The first deposition read into evidence was that of "The Widow Slater" of *Cross Creek* fame. One newspaper reported: "There was some laughter when the portly defense attorney, Sigsbee L. Scruggs, took the witness stand to read the lines of the widow."

The reading of the depositions came at the end of a long, hard day, and May was concerned that the jurors would be inattentive. He needn't have worried. Marjorie reported gratefully to Max Perkins that the jury listened to the depositions "as avidly as to the enemy's reading aloud of what they called 'lewd, lascivious, lustful and salacious' passages from *Cross Creek*." It was late Monday afternoon when they finished, and Judge Murphree recessed for the day.

On Tuesday morning, Day Seven, May decided to re-call Marjorie to the witness stand for a few last ques-tions. Had she, as Zelma claimed, paid off any of the characters in *Cross Creek*? "Not one cent." Had she ever approached Zelma or her family with an offer to settle? "No, never." And did she ask Zelma to forgive her at the time she gave her a copy of the book, as Zelma had pre-viously testified? "No, I never did. I thought there was nothing to forgive." With this, May ended his ques-tioning. Walton had no further cross-examination, and Marjorie left the witness box for the last time. May rested his case.

Walton had one final rebuttal witness to call. Zelma Cason put down her knitting and took her place on the witness stand. Did you tell the defendants' witness, Mae Dupree, that this lawsuit was "a lawyer's case," as she previously testified? Walton asked. "I did not. Emphati-cally, no." And did you, as Marjorie testified, greet her courteously in the presence of your niece on a recent oc-casion? "I am always courteous to people in my own home, or the home where I am a guest." Walton finished his questioning, and May waived cross-examination. Zelma left the witness stand and returned to her knit-ting. Walton announced to the court that he rested his re-buttal case.

At the close of all the evidence May moved for a di-rected verdict of acquittal for both defendants. There had been absolutely no evidence subjecting Norton Bas-kin to liability, he urged. And Zelma had failed to estab-lish her claims against Marjorie or prove that she had suffered any damages. Moreover, the disputed publica-tion was protected by constitutional guarantees of free speech. May's words were unavailing. Judge Murphree promptly denied the motion.

The court reconvened at 1:30 Tuesday afternoon for closing arguments. Each side was limited to two hours. Kate Walton began the argument for the plaintiff by focusing on the law of privacy. Zelma, she declared, was very shy and "doesn't even like me talking about her now but I have to." Zelma did not know about, much less consent to, Marjorie's reference to her in *Cross Creek*. The law of privacy was intended to protect "we little people, the common people," from just such unsought literary intrusions.

E. A. Clayton then took over the plaintiff's argument and drew laughter from many women in the audience when he observed: "We here in the south know what the eminent author does not know . . . that 'old maid' is a fighting term." Clayton read the objectionable passages from *Cross Creek* to the jury, noting that the truth of the description was irrelevant to the case. And despite Marjorie's success, he argued, she had no right to invade Zelma's privacy. The jury should therefore disabuse her of the notion that "the king can do no wrong." There is not, he concluded, "one law for the rich and another for the poor."

Phil May began the closing argument for the defense. He reminded the jury of Dr. Hanna's testimony concerning the literary value of *Cross Creek*. If Zelma won her case, he warned, no writer could safely write about his own life or factually portray the Florida people. All literature and news reporting would be affected. Freedom of speech would be mortally impaired. This case was unique in the annals of legal history. It represented "the first time since the invention of the printing press that an author has been forced to stand trial for a true word picture."

May's argument was scholarly and impassioned, but it was the legendary oratorical skills of Sigsbee Scruggs that stole the show. When May sat down, Sigsbee approached the jury box with assurance bred of familiarity. He knew the minds and spirits of these six men, and he knew how to win them over. One newspaper reported: "The Scruggs oratory made the hit of the day with the again-crowded courtroom, and several times the laughter was loud." Judge Murphree had to rap for order repeatedly.

Sigsbee began by warming up to the cracker jury. "Gentlemen of the jury," he began, "I'm a Florida cracker, too. My people have lived up in north Florida for a hundred years." This point won, Sigsbee turned to the case at hand. "Mr. May has given you the law," he intoned. "Now I'll give you the facts." Zelma Cason was a "self-acknowledged profane person." She was also a "public personage," subject to debate and criticism. Furthermore, Zelma was no lady of the "crinoline and old lace" period. She was a thoroughly modern woman who shouldn't be offended by the truthful statements made about her in *Cross Creek*.

Sigsbee concluded by taking the all-male jury into his confidence:

> I still get a little shocked when I see [a woman] reaching for a cigarette. . . . But I know the women of today do smoke our cigarettes, they drink our liquor, they use our language, they tell our jokes, they even wear our pants and hunt and fish beside us. It's a modern day and we must judge passages in a book such as this book by modern standards. If you fail to do so you will set us back 1,000 years.

He turned and walked deliberately back to the counsel table. The crowd murmured in appreciation.

It was J. V. Walton, though, who had the final word. Presenting the plaintiff's rebuttal argument, he challenged the literary merit of *Cross Creek*. Descriptions of animal mating habits were not part of a legitimate picture of Florida, he argued, but were included to sell the book. The portrayal of "my profane friend Zelma" was malicious, because Marjorie singled Zelma out of a number of colorful characters who could have been described in the same way. And Marjorie's fame as a writer was completely irrelevant: "To hold that things like this can be written because the writer is an eminent author is like holding that Joe Louis could come down here and knock down the ordinary citizen just because he is world's champion."

It was now time for Judge Murphree to have his moment in the spotlight. It was late Tuesday afternoon when he began to read aloud his fifteen-page charge to the jury. The judge quoted extensively from the allegations of Zelma's declaration and Marjorie's responsive pleading, explaining their legal import to the jurors. He told them that they could take their copies of *Cross Creek* to the jury room to aid in their deliberations. He then instructed the bailiff to escort the jurors out of the courtroom. It was approximately 6:30 P.M. on May 28, 1946—one day before Zelma's fifty-sixth birthday.

Marjorie and her lawyers remained in the courtroom, as did many of the spectators and reporters, in the hope that the jury would reach a verdict quickly. Zelma pushed her way out through the crowd, holding her knitting bag up to her face. So when the jury returned at about 7:00 P.M. after only 28 minutes of deliberation, Zelma was not on hand to hear their verdict: "We, the jury, find the defendants, Marjorie Kinnan Baskin and Norton Baskin, her husband, not guilty. So say we all."

The courtroom was pandemonium. The crowd applauded wildly and pressed forward to congratulate Marjorie. The jurors were surrounded by well-wishers, who pumped their hands in appreciation. Marjorie clung to her husband's arm and struggled to maintain her composure as she greeted the happy throng. She made only one comment: "I'm glad that a jury has upheld a principle of factual writing." J. H. White spoke for his fellow jurors: "We just didn't believe this had gone beyond free speech and had invaded private rights," he said. The other jurors nodded their heads in agreement.

Marjorie and Norton left the courthouse and returned to Cross Creek. They were accompanied this time by a small group of lawyers, friends, and newspaper reporters. The happy party celebrated late into the night, reviewing the week's events and rejoicing over the jury's verdict.

Marjorie was exhilarated and exhausted at the same time. After three years of worried distraction over the lawsuit, she could now savor the sweet taste of victory. She wrote triumphantly to Max Perkins:

> The trial vindicated, to me, two things: the democratic system, for I felt that if that most commonplace jury, none of whom had ever read anything I had written, could not see that something important was involved, there was no hope; and the loyalty and friendship of all the people, their integrity, of which I had written so many years.

Marjorie was bright enough to realize that the fight wasn't over yet. But on the night of her grand victory, surrounded by friends and fired with new hope, the possibility of renewed warfare seemed remote indeed. That was tomorrow's problem.

Chapter Eight

A Hollow Victory

Few people were as entitled to self-congratulation in the days following the *Cross Creek* trial as Marjorie and Phil May. They had manned the front line of battle together for over three years, consulting, commiserating, and encouraging each other under the most trying circumstances. Now, in the glow of their legal triumph, the two heaped praise on each other in almost embarrassing quantity.

The day after the jury's verdict was handed down, May wrote to Marjorie in his own hand: "No other achievement in my professional life has brought as much gratification as has the victory in the Cross Creek case. . . . You are a very satisfactory client. So few of my women clients are." Marjorie—ignoring for the moment the slur on her sex—responded with heartfelt thanks: "I should have been wretched in any other hands but yours. You have a rare integrity, and I am grateful to have had it used in my behalf." May wrote to Marjorie again in almost mystical tones: "I came to feel that I was an instrument of destiny and that a force greater than the sum of the minds and hearts of the individuals involved was guiding the course of events to your ultimate vindication." He concluded with religious fervor:

> The attack which Walton made on the book revealed to me values in it which I had missed. I had considered The Yearling your best work. Now I know that it is Cross Creek. You show how to know life as it really is and find it good and beautiful. I

might well have gathered that before from the grateful reader who gave *Cross Creek* the place on her bedside table which had long been occupied by the Bible.

Letters also poured in from Marjorie's publisher, her fellow writers, and the public. Typical of the accolades received was a letter from a woman who had attended the trial:

> I am delighted that Zelma got nothing out of her suit against you—nothing except all the sweaters she knitted. And I hope *they* don't fit! She's worse than Madam Defarge. . . . I hope having *Cross Creek* under fire will cause a great boom in sales again, and pay you somewhat for the exhausting experience of that trial.

The possibility of a boost to book sales had not gone unnoticed by Marjorie and Phil May. Zelma had done more to publicize *Cross Creek* than Scribner's could ever have done. If the publicity renewed the buying public's interest, at least something might be salvaged from the wreckage of this exhausting ordeal. Three days after the verdict May wrote to Scribner's business manager Whitney Darrow, inquiring whether the publicity had resulted in increased book sales. Darrow responded with a list of disappointing national sales figures. He later wrote with more encouraging news. There had been an increase in sales of the reprint edition in Florida, one bookseller reporting: "Naturally it is a choice piece of gossip here, and everyone wants to read the book." Among the new *Cross Creek* buyers was Judge Murphree, who was spotted purchasing the book in a Gainesville bookstore.

Marjorie's growing dismay at post-trial events involved more than concern over flagging book sales. She was deeply disturbed that the national press failed to recognize the significance of her victory. Now that the hoopla of the trial had died down, the press seemed apathetic to the real point of the case—the vindication of the rights of authors. Marjorie was grieved to hear the news conveyed by Darrow in early June: Scribner's agents had traveled to five American cities and had heard not a word about the trial in the press or literary circles. Darrow succeeded in persuading *Publishers Weekly* to do an article, but that did little to offset Marjorie's disappointment when only two brief notices about the case appeared in the New York City newspapers.

There was a short blurb about the lawsuit in the "People" section of the June 10, 1946, *Time Magazine*, in which Marjorie was described as being "finally free" of the lawsuit. Marjorie shot a lengthy letter back to the *Time* editors, protesting that she was not yet free of possible legal appeals nor did she wish to be as long as there was any threat to artistic freedom. She seized the opportunity to vent her growing frustration:

> I was surprised that there was practically nothing about the case outside of Florida newspapers, for a vital principle is involved: the right of anyone to write of his or her own life, where that necessarily involves mention of other people, short, of course, of libel. . . . I bring all this to your attention, as thinking that you may be interested in following this peculiar case through to its end, for the same reason as has motivated me to fight it so long and so hard and so expensively, i.e., the basic freedom of the press in general.

Marjorie's sense of isolation was compounded by Scribner's apparent indifference. Though Whitney Darrow responded to May's occasional requests for information, and Max Perkins continued to write his loving and heartfelt letters to Marjorie, it was obvious that they didn't share her vital concern for the case. On the afternoon of May 28, 1946, the day of the verdict, Marjorie received telegrams from both Darrow and Perkins indicating that they had only just learned the trial was in progress. Darrow later wrote to May: "Unfortunately, no one here knew anything at all about the trial until after it was far along."

For over three years, Marjorie had withstood the heat of battle. And her ordeal was not over yet. In June of 1946, Zelma filed a motion for a new trial listing sixty-six grounds of error. On July 15 Kate Walton argued the motion in a two-and-a-half-hour hearing before Judge Murphree, during what Phil May described as "the hottest day Gainesville has ever known." Judge Murphree denied the motion, and Marjorie knew that a second appeal to the Florida Supreme Court was imminent.

Amidst this renewed paper war came another unwelcome distraction. Marjorie had never been as close to Sigsbee Scruggs as she was to Phil May. Now a dispute over Sigsbee's fees threatened to rupture their admiring but distant relationship. Sigsbee had originally agreed to assist May for a fee of $350, believing that his services would be limited to interviewing a few witnesses, selecting the jury, and sitting in on a three-day trial. His role turned out to be larger than anticipated, and the trial longer.

By early June it was obvious that a dispute over legal fees was brewing. In July Sigsbee informed May that he and Parks Carmichael had provided fourteen-and-a-half days of legal services at the usual rate of $100 per day, for a total fee of $1,450, but that he would be willing to settle for $1,350. Marjorie, May, and Sigsbee exchanged a flurry of polite but cool letters. May wrote to Sigsbee that he felt his charges were excessive, and that he, May, would not be charging as much as $50 per day. Privately, though, he encouraged Marjorie to swallow her pride and pay Sigsbee what he wanted, rather than "have a scrap with him."

Marjorie finally capitulated, but she couldn't resist one last, gentle jab:

> I enclose my check . . . and with it, my thanks for your very fine help during the trial, and your splendid argument to the jury. . . . I must admit that the rate of payment you receive for your professional work is higher than the rate I receive for mine. However, I suppose that, like a doctor, you feel obliged to handle so many cases for poor people, who can pay only a minimum, or nothing at all, that you must necessarily make it up on those who can afford higher fees.

Sigsbee was appeased, and he agreed to appear gratis at an upcoming hearing on the taxation of court costs. He and Marjorie retained a veneer of polite cooperation, but resentment lingered. May, for his part, commented: "It costs like hell to defend a principle!"

Unfortunately, the cost to Marjorie was more than just money. She had borne up stoically during the protracted legal battle. Her correspondence during these years with friends and literary associates was remarkable for its infrequent mention of the lawsuit. Writer A.J. Cronin commended Marjorie on her stamina after the trial:

> I think you showed great courage in bearing up as you did and, more significant still, in saying so little about it. . . . There is something of the stoic in you and I can imagine that stinging vipers and Florida juries might venomously assail you without eliciting so much as a whimper.

But those closest to Marjorie knew that the case was a

drain on her emotional and physical resources, and they were worried.

May was deeply concerned about the effect of the protracted lawsuit on his stalwart client. He marveled at Marjorie's strength during the trial, but he wasn't surprised when she suffered a "nervous reaction" after it was over. He wrote to her in mid-June: "I am sorry that the nervous reaction which I feared for you finally came. You gave no sign of its approach during the trial. I never observed greater poise than you displayed." Two months later Marjorie disclosed that she was still suffering the effects of the trial:

> This morning I thought I was going to be very ill, then suddenly realized that it is just nervous exhaustion brought on, or rather, protracted, by this goddam law suit. It would cure Zelma's ulcers permanently if she knew what she had done to me.

Max Perkins was also concerned about Marjorie's reaction. A month after the trial he wrote: "I knew that the trial had been a great strain upon you. Though you went through it beautifully, it must have been exhausting, and people who have that quality of rising to an occasion, do their suffering afterward." Marjorie conceded that the lawsuit had taken its toll. "Well, it is over," she wrote to Perkins, "and I hope to get down to hard work."

Zelma's lawsuit has been widely blamed for the decline in Marjorie's productivity during the last decade of her life. Marjorie believed this herself, at times. To a friend she wrote: "So [the lawsuit] drags on and on, and has it interfered with my work!" But it is tempting to overemphasize the impact of the suit on Marjorie's creative life. There were other pressures that were as much, or more, to blame for the disruption of her literary output. The lawsuit was only part of the story.

Marjorie's special anguish during the period from 1943

to 1953 was the painful labor of producing her last novel, *The Sojourner*, published a few months before her death in 1953. It was her only major work since the publication of *Cross Creek*, and it took nearly ten years to finish. Marjorie fervently wished to write a book of more universal theme, without the anchor of the Florida scene and dialect. *The Sojourner*, the symbolic saga of a northern farmer and his noble struggle with materialism, would be this book. Marjorie worked on it fitfully and despairingly.

Marjorie poured out her frustrations to friends and colleagues, but she did not blame the lawsuit for her lack of progress on the novel. In April of 1945 she wrote to Max Perkins: "In the winter, I made still another start on the book, and it was wrong, too. Part of the trouble, of course, is that something is still not right with my conception." To writer Ellen Glasgow she wrote in November: "I am in a dreadful state of mind, from being unable to do anything with a novel that has been long on my mind, and on which I have made eight or nine beginnings.... I don't know what's wrong." She was still making false starts on the novel nine months after the trial. She confided to Perkins: "I have never felt more inadequate." Nearly six years after the trial she was still struggling. "I have abandoned poor dear Norton once again to tuck in at Cross Creek to finish that bloody book," she wrote to a friend.

Marjorie was encouraged and cajoled by her literary friends. A particularly persistent voice of concern was Virginia author James Branch Cabell. Shortly after the trial Cabell wrote to Marjorie:

Nobody knows better than I the strain to which you have been subjected ... and the difficulty in such circumstances of doing any writing. I saw the effects of it on you, but I could only sympathize in silence, without insulting your intelligence by telling you not to worry.... I exhort you to get back to work steadfastly.

Three years and many letters later he was still exhorting:

I hope you are making progress with that so long promised book. I think it is a crime the way you have backed and filled about writing this novel, as indeed I believe I have mentioned some odd dozens of times.

Apart from her anguish over *The Sojourner*, another major distraction for Marjorie was World War II. Marjorie shared her sorrow with writer Ellen Glasgow: "The burden of war is inescapable, I think, and a great pressure from it seems to weigh on whatever else one is battling, mental or physical." And then, in July of 1943, Norton Baskin volunteered to serve as an ambulance driver with the American Field Service. He was sent to India, and Marjorie worried about his health and safety. She wrote Glasgow that she was unable to settle down to work on *The Sojourner*, because she was "more disturbed about my husband than I will admit." In January of 1944 she was "in sort of a fog" upon learning that Norton was in battle action. Four months later she wrote to Max Perkins: "I have never taken such a beating as in the last few weeks ... not knowing whether Norton was dead or alive."

At the same time she was fretting over Norton's safety, Marjorie was also anxiously awaiting the Florida Supreme Court's decision on Zelma's first appeal. Then came a tragic fire at Norton's Castle Warden Hotel in St. Augustine in which two women were killed. Norton was sent home desperately ill after nearly a year-and-a-half of service, and Marjorie nursed him through the debilitating effects of amoebic dysentery.

Even the happiness of Marjorie's marriage was a significant distraction from her writing. Her time was divided between Cross Creek and St. Augustine, and her fame and love of good company increased her social obligations. She complained to a friend:

> [T]he conflict between trying to be a writer and good wife at the same time does disturb me, as the one calls for a completely hermit existence, and the other for gregariousness (which I enjoy when I'm through with a job of writing).

The practical demands on Marjorie's time increased when, in the summer of 1947, she took on the burden of another residence. She had vacationed in Van Hornesville, New York, at the invitation of friends, who hoped that the northern setting would encourage Marjorie in her work on *The Sojourner*. Marjorie found the area so congenial that she decided to purchase and renovate an old farmhouse. There she spent the next few summers laboring to complete her book, worrying about Norton back in Florida, and trying from afar to keep track of the cows, chickens, and other mundane details of life at Cross Creek, "my true home."

The move to Van Hornesville coincided with a devastating loss. In June 1947 Marjorie learned of the death of her editor and friend, Max Perkins. This misfortune overwhelmed her. Marjorie and Perkins had corresponded at a rare level of intimacy for a decade and a half. Perkins's death meant the end of his priceless literary advice and encouragement. How could she go on with this impossible book without Max to guide her? Marjorie poured out her emotions in a letter written from Van Hornesville to her friend, poet Bernice Gilkyson:

The night we reached here ... Charlie's telegram about Max's death was handed to me. I felt like turning right around and going home again, as it seemed the last straw of impossibility to try to get the book going, without Max. It was startling to realize ... how much we wrote *for* him, and certainly with his judgment constantly in mind. I dream about him often and wake up in tears.

Marjorie's creative concerns were compounded by worrisome physical problems, and each fed on the other. Repeated hospitalizations and surgeries during the last years of her life took critical time and energies away from her writing; the emotional torment caused by her lack of productivity contributed to the physical symptoms. She continued to drive herself to create, against advice. But still she went on, with that peculiar artist's urge, while the peace of mind that should have come with her remarkable previous success continued to evade her. The year before her death she wrote to Jack Wheelock, her new editor at Scribner's:

I am exhausted mentally, emotionally, spiritually ... it's absurd that anything good should come out of me, and I can never believe that it does, because the process is so anguished and *messy*. ... I live a life, not of Thoreau's quiet desperation, but of overt and blatant desperation.

So Marjorie's life during and after the *Cross Creek* trial was filled with hardships that contributed to her creative decline. And yet, there were times when her legal problems seemed to engulf all others. She wrote to a friend in 1949: "[T]he law suit crushed me—the triumphant ending, with all of Cross Creek rallying to my support, did not quite compensate for the anguish." Once she even told Phil May that she would no longer write about her beloved Florida, so frustrated was she by the suit. May urged her to drop such ridiculous notions:

It was disappointing and distressing for me to hear you say that you did not intend to produce any more writings with a Florida background. . . . It is my firm conviction that the spiritual force, in which I believe but do not attempt to identify, guided you to Florida to know and write sympathetically of it and its people so that all of us would be encouraged in the conviction that there is always beauty in life for those who seek it.

Marjorie never did write another book about Florida, but it was her untimely death, rather than Zelma's lawsuit, that was to blame. She continued to collect stories about Cross Creek, and she nurtured a plan to write a sequel called *Death at the Creek*. Marjorie first hinted at her intentions in a June 1947 letter to Phil May. She brought up the subject again over a year later, after a short but idyllic stay at Cross Creek: "I found myself making notes all summer for new 'Cross Creek' chapters," she wrote. "Many of them are sad, as there have been nearly a dozen deaths since the book was written, and several strange tragedies, as well." She also asked May if she could write freely about the *Cross Creek* trial. May replied that he was "delighted" with her new enthusiasm, and she need have no fear about invasion of privacy: "There is nothing that I know about more completely in the public domain than is a law suit which has been finally determined."

Marjorie died before *Death at the Creek* was written, but her plans for the book showed that the trial had not doused the creative flame lit by Cross Creek. And despite her moments of angry frustration, she retained an affection and joyous vitality rooted in her love for the Creek. In 1947 she wrote to a friend:

I wish to report that my status at Cross Creek and environs is quite unchanged. I have already been *embraced* by five of my women friends in the neighborhood, usually most undemonstrative, and had my hand pumped by as many or more men, all expressing joy that I am "home." You see, they all *know* that this is home to me, and understand that my being away is due only to the accidental misfortune of having fallen in love with a hotel man. These people don't change. . . . They would do anything in the world for me, and I for them, and we all know this.

Perhaps the other distractions in her life—and the happy distraction of her homecomings to Cross Creek —helped to numb Marjorie against the continuing pain of the lawsuit. For though the trial was now blessedly behind her, Marjorie's battles were far from over. Two more years would pass before the last legal maneuver was exhausted and the case put to rest. In the meantime, Marjorie continued her voluminous correspondence with May, and May continued his devoted ministrations. He had little choice. On September 14, 1946, Zelma filed her second notice of appeal to the Florida Supreme Court.

Chapter Nine

The Battle Won, the War Lost

While Marjorie and Phil May were enjoying a brief respite after their courtroom victory, Zelma and her lawyers were hard at work. The raucous trial, the public exposure of her quirks and tantrums, and the short jury deliberation steeled the resolve of the steely Zelma Cason. She would see this thing through to the bitter end.

Kate Walton was with her all the way. After Judge Murphree denied Kate's motion for a new trial, she decided on another plan of attack. She filed a motion challenging the validity of the final judgment itself, arguing in yet another hearing before a tired Judge Murphree that the judgment was improperly entered by the clerk. The parties agreed to the entry of a new final judgment effective July 16, 1946, giving Kate some additional time within which to prepare her appeal. The notice of appeal, signed by Kate Walton and E. A. Clayton, was filed within the sixty-day period required by court rule. The battle lines were drawn again.

In this second appeal Kate alleged thirty-nine grounds for reversal of the jury's verdict, ranging from errors in jury selection to errors in the court's final judgment. Kate's forty-four-page appellant's brief was described by the Rawlings camp as "both a remarkable and difficult document." May labored studiously over his own forty-page appellees' brief, which received high praise from both Marjorie and Sigsbee Scruggs. On April 10, 1947, Kate Walton and Phil May argued this second appeal before the Florida Supreme Court.

The appeal was heard by six of the seven justices. The seventh justice—one of two who dissented in Marjorie's favor in the first appeal—was ill. May was disturbed by some of the questions asked by the justices during his oral argument, and two days later he sent a lengthy letter to the court containing additional argument. May stressed the damaging consequences of a reversal:

> The decision in this case will make judicial history as did the decision on the first appeal. The consequences upon future publications will be far reaching. . . . Books can not be written unless authors are free to weave into their writings, directly or indirectly, their experiences, their friends, and acquaintances.

On May 23, 1947, the Florida Supreme Court handed down its decision. In an opinion authored by Justice Chillingworth, the court held that Zelma had proven her case for invasion of privacy and was entitled to judgment in her favor. It rejected the defendants' claim that Zelma was a public figure who had relinquished her right of privacy. The court declared that Marjorie's fame was completely irrelevant to the case, and that Judge Murphree had wrongfully admitted "a great mass of immaterial and prejudicial evidence." The court hit hard on what had been the heart of Marjorie's defense:

> Personal rights of the plaintiff are not to be tested by the status or identity of the defendant. The whole force and trend of the defendant's evidence was to exalt and praise the defendant and to establish her great prominence—when that was not an issue in the case. No legitimate or general public interest in the defendant alone can justify an invasion of the right of privacy of another, who has in no sense of the word consented to that invasion or waived her rights.

The Florida Supreme Court hears the appeal

We, therefore, conclude that this evidence was prejudicial to a fair trial of this cause. It tended to confuse the jury and withdraw its consideration from the issue as to whether or not the plaintiff was one concerning whom there was a general and legitimate public interest, rather than defendant. Hence the judgment for the defendant should be reversed.

The court went on to find, however, that Zelma had failed to prove she had been injured by the publication of *Cross Creek*. Her health was not impaired, and she had even gained weight. Zelma's testimony did not support a finding that she had suffered mental anguish or that Marjorie had acted with malice. So, while "the evidence vindicates plaintiff, in establishing a wrongful invasion of her right of privacy," she was not entitled to recover actual or punitive damages. The court therefore reversed the judgment in Marjorie's favor and ordered a new trial, with directions that Zelma recover only nominal damages and costs.

The decision came as a real blow to Marjorie and Phil May. Never mind that Zelma was awarded only nominal damages. The real point of their struggle—the vindication of authors' freedom to write—had been lost. May wrote Marjorie that the decision was "a great shock and disappointment.... I never before handled a case in which I had greater confidence." Max Perkins consoled Marjorie in what was probably his last letter to her before his death: "This is just a line to say how deeply I sympathize with you in the outcome of the appeal. It all seems utterly mysterious to me.... It is very much too bad."

May had a more personal reason to be dismayed at the decision. He was a close friend of Justice Chillingworth (whom he called "Chick"), the author of the hard-hitting opinion. May was stung by the opinion's criticism of the defense tactics at trial. He later vented his frustrations in a letter to Judge Murphree, who also was stung by the criticism of his rulings on admission of evidence:

> It was puzzling to me to determine how a man of [Justice Chillingworth's] good judgment and usual restraint could have written so flippantly and unjudicially of the conduct of a trial.... Appellate judges live in ivory towers. They are human beings and will occasionally exhibit their authority in a flippant and unjudicial manner.

Marjorie immediately insisted that the case be appealed to the United States Supreme Court, a course of action May felt was unavailable under current procedural rules. He even advised against filing a petition for re-hearing with the Florida Supreme Court. He feared that the court might decide to remand the case for a full trial, a real risk with their primary defense gone and no holds barred on damages. Whitney Darrow also tried to discourage Marjorie from considering a further appeal, reminding her that it would be time-consuming, costly, and possibly fruitless.

Marjorie wasn't the only litigant unhappy with the court's decision. Zelma Cason's famous profanity was being privately tested as she brooded on the matter. The award of nominal damages made Zelma's legal victory seem hollow. Marjorie puzzled over Zelma's negative reaction to the decision. She wrote to May:

> I wrote Norton that having lost my fight for a principle, I couldn't help wishing that Zelma would take it as a moral victory for *her*. Afterward, I thought, "What a simple-minded fool I am! She doesn't give a damn about a moral victory. She wants the cash!"

Both sides seemed confused by the court's decision. What step was next, and who had to take it? Kate Walton filed a petition for re-hearing, which the court denied on June 20, 1947. May (hoping to avoid a large monetary award) then took the position that Judge Murphree should simply enter judgment in Zelma's favor for $1.00 and the usual court costs, without another trial. Kate Walton wrote the Chief Justice of the Florida Supreme Court a letter, hoping to obtain more specific directions. Months of inaction passed.

In January of 1948 Kate filed an unprecedented motion for clarification, asking the court to clarify what it meant by the award of "all costs" and "nominal damages." In the motion Kate referred to a piece of "newly discovered evidence of malice" that she hoped to introduce in a new trial: a letter from Marjorie to Zelma in September of 1933 "plainly admitting her knowledge of the deep and irreparable breach in her former friendly relations with plaintiff, which said letter directly contradicts the sworn testimony of defendant author at the trial."

Marjorie recalled writing such a conciliatory letter, but she assured May this did not contradict her trial testimony that she did not believe the friendship was breached. She was outraged by the attack on her integrity:

If *you* are puzzled by the so-called "legal" goings-on, imagine how I feel! It is all quite beyond me. It does seem to me utterly outrageous that with a case supposedly ended, Kate Walton should be allowed to make an unwarranted attack on me, practically accusing me of perjury. . . . Have we no redress against such a vicious thing as Kate's charge?

On January 12 the Florida Supreme Court denied Kate's motion for clarification. The next day J. V. Walton suffered a heart attack, and Kate obtained May's permission to delay further action. For several months the case brewed, with Marjorie's camp believing that Zelma's camp was regrouping for renewed battle.

The delay renewed Marjorie's interest in an appeal to the United States Supreme Court. In March of 1948 she was encouraged by a reporter from the *Miami Herald*, who told her that his newspaper might help to pay for an appeal because of the important free speech issue at stake. Marjorie raised the subject of financial assistance with Whitney Darrow, hoping that Scribner's might at last see the light. "[Y]ou would have thought I'd dropped an ice-cube down his neck," she reported to May. May valiantly offered to donate his services for nothing, but both he and Marjorie knew the appeal was a pipe dream. There was neither a legal nor a financial basis to continue. "It is doubtful whether I can afford to put any more money into it," Marjorie conceded sorrowfully. "Oh Phil, I *do* want to go on to the Supreme Court. I have never taken the easy way out and cannot bear to begin now."

The hardest part of all was deciding whether to be pleased or dismayed by the outcome of the second appeal. Marjorie and May vacillated between feelings of failure and occasional flickers of pride when others managed to convince them that they deserved congratulations. But the feelings of failure usually prevailed. Marjorie wrote to May sardonically that she had had a "violent argument" with two friends—one a member of the New York bar—who insisted that Marjorie had indeed been triumphant. Marjorie had conceded to her friends that the jury's verdict was a "local vindication," but she held fast to the conviction that she had lost the all-important fight for principle. May responded that his lawyer friends were trying to convince him of the same thing, but "[t]o me, as ... to you, there is small consolation in the fact that Zelma and Kate Walton have derived no profit from ... the case."

In one of her really low moments, Marjorie even composed a letter to the justices of the Florida Supreme Court:

Gentlemen:

My health is not of the best, and I am not getting any younger, and it has been in my mind, due largely to an enormous number of requests from readers of my book "Cross Creek," to continue my autobiographical study of my life in the locale of the book.

Unfinished stories have found an end, new and touching relationships have developed, since I began the actual writing of the book about eight years ago. The war also changed our lives.

I am wondering if it is pertinent or impertinent for me to ask Your Honors' advice as to whether it is legally permissible to write such a book of personal memoirs. If the Florida law requires that I get permission in advance from each of the individuals concerned in my life story, or to pay, or agree to pay, something to each of them, it will make an almost impossible undertaking. Some of my friends and neighbors of whom I wrote previously, have died, but have heirs and descendants. Some have moved far away, with no known addresses.

My attorneys feel unable to advise me in this matter.

Begging the indulgence of your consideration.

Marjorie Kinnan Rawlings

Marjorie shared a copy of the letter with May, commenting that she would "love" to send it on to the court. But she realized it would be "sheer impertinence" to do so. The letter remained safely tucked away in May's files.

It all ended with a whimper instead of a bang. In July

of 1948 Kate Walton wrote to May proposing that the parties stipulate to the entry of judgment for nominal damages of $1.00 and court costs of $1,050.10. May and Marjorie reluctantly agreed. Kate did not, however, want Judge Murphree to handle the final hearing. She wrote him a letter urging him to withdraw from the case due to his "admiration for Mrs. Baskin," his tolerance of "the disorderly audience" at trial, and his admission of evidence "to inflame and prejudice the jury."

In the end Kate capitulated and agreed to drop her objection to Judge Murphree. On August 9, 1948, outside the glare of the public and press, Kate and May appeared before him and quietly consented to the entry of final judgment. Marjorie promptly sent a check for the amount to the clerk, and the judgment was marked "satisfied." Five-and-a-half years after the the filing of Zelma's declaration, the ink dried on the last legal document. The case of *Zelma Cason v. Marjorie Kinnan Baskin* was legal history.

As the lawsuit wound down to its inexorable, undramatic end, Marjorie resigned herself to defeat. As usual, she poured out her deepest feelings to May, in a letter penned the day after the final judgment was entered:

Dear Phil:

I know. I have failed you. I should have fought it out to the bitter end. We might have had a chance of reaching the United States Supreme Court. Do you know what made me decide to "end it all"? It was the comment made to Norton by my friend Edith Pope. If a fellow Florida writer thought I *had* invaded Zelma's privacy ... it suddenly did not seem worth while to carry on the battle. My own personal vindication came in the Gainesville courtroom, as you have reminded me.

I wonder if by any chance I have given you the impression that I felt you had failed in any way. I

The final judgment

do not. No one could have done a more superb job, have kept the whole business on a higher plane, than you. My only reproaches are for myself, for not having seen it through, as I swore to do. But I am becoming almost dangerously frustrated at not getting my book going. Years more of conflict might make the book impossible to do. And without my writing, I am nothing. . . .

My fury is all for the members of the Florida Supreme Court who took a small-range point of view. . . . The failure is not yours. . . . There is a type of mind that is *incapable* of understanding.

Have you read Lecomte du Nouy's "Human Destiny"? If not, you *must* do so. . . . You will find an application, and a comfort, for our defeat. For . . . you and I know privately that we *were* defeated. But I shall be most miserable if you take any blame to yourself.

With admiration and affection,

Marjorie

But Marjorie was not yet to have the luxury of critical reflection on a closed case. Just when it seemed that the lawsuit was finally put to rest, there was one last, unexpected flare-up. On August 9, 1948, in the letter acknowledging Marjorie's satisfaction of the judgment for court costs, Kate Walton dropped a bombshell. She wrote to May: "Miss Cason would like Mrs. Baskin's assurance and the assurance of Scribner's that the objectionable depiction of her will not be further published." May immediately notified Scribner's of this "surprising, disappointing and disturbing development." Scribner's consulted its attorney, who agreed with May that the demand was groundless, because it had not been made part of the final settlement. Zelma had never tried to enjoin publication of the book; she had only claimed monetary damages.

Marjorie reacted at first with "horrified surprise" to Kate's demand. Then her impish mind conceived a new plan: If Zelma insisted on being deleted from *Cross Creek*, so be it. In future editions of the book Marjorie would keep everything the way it was, substituting "my friend Jakey" for "my friend Zelma." She wrote to May: "Zelma's inflated ego is having her gloating, I know, thinking that she is throwing us all into utter confusion."

In the end, Marjorie and May decided to simply ignore Zelma's demand. Marjorie continued to toy with the idea of deleting Zelma altogether from the book, but she soon dropped the notion. There were only small sales of the reprint edition now. And after all, "my friend Zelma" was as indelibly printed on the minds of the reading public as on the pages of *Cross Creek*.

Now the lawsuit began to fade from Marjorie's day-to-day concerns and from her letters to May. In November of 1948 she spent several days at Cross Creek, cleaning and repairing the old homestead. And she began to write again, making notes for new *Cross Creek* chapters. She wrote to May: "All my pettishness has melted away under the old spell, and I am sick at heart at having to leave. I shall never be truly happy until I can live here again. It *must* come about."

It had all come full circle. Marjorie was home again. Nothing, really, had changed.

Epilogue

Friends

Life in Cross Creek and Island Grove returned pretty much to normal after that. Not that these twin communities were especially impressed by the legal goings-on anyway. Gainesville had been more excited about the noise and celebrity of the trial than Marjorie's cracker neighbors had ever been. After all, the world-famous author had lived and written in their midst for over twenty years and was as close to being one of them as a Yankee could be. For them, the personal feud between neighbors was the real trouble, and even this had rippled the waters of peaceful co-existence only slightly.

Despite her fondest hopes, Marjorie returned to her beloved Cross Creek less frequently as the trial faded from memory. Her agonized struggle to complete *The Sojourner* and the stewardship of her homes in New York and St. Augustine called Marjorie away from the old farmhouse at Cross Creek. But she was always there in spirit, and interspersed with her letters to literary greats were letters to friends at Cross Creek, exhorting them on the care of chickens, grove, and fences.

In the last year of her life, spurning evidence of mental and physical fatigue, Marjorie plunged into a new work—the biography of writer Ellen Glasgow. She spent months of research in Virginia, conducting interviews and gathering notes with new enthusiasm and energy. The book would never be completed. Marjorie suffered a cerebral hemorrhage at her beach cottage near St. Augustine on the morning of December 14, 1953. She died that evening.

After the trial Zelma continued her job with the State Welfare Department, working out of St. Augustine and returning home often to Island Grove. She and Kate Walton remained good friends. For a while Zelma had some hard feelings toward her neighbors. So many of them had testified for Marjorie. None of the Cason family showed up at the funeral for Mrs. Noel Moore, wife of Island Grove's deputy sheriff, who died just days after the trial. But nobody really believed the rumors that the Casons were trying to sell their house in Island Grove. And they never did. Mrs. Cason lived there until her death, and today it is still owned by members of the Cason family.

Marjorie and Zelma did not meet again for some time after Zelma strode angrily out of the Gainesville courtroom. Then one day in St. Augustine, two or three years after the trial, Marjorie came home and told Norton that she had run into Zelma at a florist shop. When Marjorie walked in, Zelma was in the back of the shop. The two "fell into each other's arms." Marjorie said, "Zelma, you know I wouldn't do anything to hurt you." And Zelma said, "I know, honey. It was those old lawyers, not me. I would never do anything to hurt you either." Marjorie told her husband that she didn't plan to see Zelma regularly, but she was glad for the chance encounter: "I'd rather have her as a friend than an enemy."

Though she was never completely happy with her portrayal in *Cross Creek*, Zelma found it in her heart to forgive Marjorie for the real or imagined injuries she had caused her. Zelma's co-worker Alice Ellis said that Zelma often talked of Marjorie in the years after the trial:

> I don't know how long after the trial—maybe it was several years—that I realized that Zelma and Marge were visiting. I asked her if she was still mad

at Marge and she said "no." Definitely before Marge died, Zelma and Marge were friends again.

Zelma even came to regret her role in the lawsuit, though she never publicly admitted it. She was heard to remark in private, sadly rather than proudly: "I'm the bitch that sued Marjorie." In 1953 she wept upon hearing about Marjorie's death, and she joined other friends at the funeral.

Zelma lived on another ten years after Marjorie's death. In 1960 she suffered a stroke and was eventually moved to a nursing facility in St. Augustine. She began to hallucinate, often talking about Marjorie. Norton Baskin went to visit her, and he told her "that Marjorie had never had any bitterness, that it was only a question of the right to write." He also sent her flowers every Christmas and Easter. The first Christmas he sent her a large poinsettia, inscribing the card, "From Norton, and indirectly, from Marjorie." After that, Zelma always believed that the flowers came from Marjorie. She told a friend, "I know [the card] says Norton, but Marjorie is the one sending these. Now I know that she is all right with me."

Zelma died in 1963 and was buried in the isolated Antioch Cemetery near Island Grove, among such familiar names as Tom Morrison, Annie Slater, and George Fairbanks. Fifty feet to the west of the Cason plot is another familiar name. Set in the flat, sandy earth is a simple stone, bearing the following inscription:

Marjorie Kinnan Rawlings
Wife of Norton Baskin.

Through Her Writings She Endeared
Herself to the People of the World.

Marjorie's burial at Antioch Cemetery, often the source of ironic comment, was an accident. Marjorie had asked to be buried in the Citra cemetery, south of Island Grove, where neighbor Tom Glisson was buried. But after Marjorie died, the wrong instructions were given to the funeral director. Norton Baskin realized a mistake had been made only when the funeral procession drove toward Antioch Cemetery. "I hated to make a last-minute fuss," he recalled. "She had friends buried at Antioch, too." So the occasional visitor to this unimposing cemetery marvels to find that Marjorie and Zelma have achieved in death what they weren't quite able to accomplish in life—peaceful co-existence.

Marjorie's funeral was as modest as her final resting place. At Norton's request, Phil May gave a short tribute at the end of the service. With his usual insight, he decided to let Marjorie's words speak for themselves. He picked up a copy of *Cross Creek* and read aloud the last paragraph, the one that had been his particular favorite: "Who owns Cross Creek? The red-birds, I think, more than I. . . . Cross Creek belongs to the wind and the rain, to the sun and the seasons, to the cosmic secrecy of seed, and beyond all, to time."

Among the many flowers from friends and admirers was a special arrangement sent by Marjorie's neighbors at the Creek. The names of the contributors read like the pages of *Cross Creek:* Fairbanks, Townsend, Slater, Glisson. It was because of such friends—these solid, proud people—that Marjorie had come to the Creek, stayed there during hard times, written so lovingly about it, endured the rigors of trial, and emerged with her sense of community intact.

A letter came with the flowers, addressed to Norton Baskin. Its words bridged the currents of time, grief, and memory. It said simply:

Dear Mr. Baskin —

We are sending a list of those who helped in the Flower arrangements. We all have a verry deep regret and a feeling of looseing someone verry dear to us. I know that your grief is beyond words, but I can truthfully say that you have friends and Friends of Miss Rawlings at Cross Creek who shairs your grief with you. Hope you can stop by with us if not but a few minutes when you come over here. We are just the same as ever.

Friends.

Notes

The left-hand column identifies first the page number, then the line number, to which these notes pertain.

Prologue. Meeting on the Bridge

1, 21 M. Rawlings, *Cross Creek* (New York: Charles Scribner's Sons,1942), p. 365; hereafter, "*Cross Creek*"[1]

2, 11 Trial Transcript (hereafter, "T.T."), vol. III, p. 346 (testimony of MKR)[2]

2, 20 *Cross Creek*, p. 38

2, 35 T.T., vol. III, p. 272 (testimony of MKR)

Chapter 1. A Love Story

5, 6 Letter from MKR to Philip S. May, July 2, 1945, reproduced in G. Bigelow and L. Monti, *Selected*

---

1. The name of Marjorie Kinnan Rawlings is abbreviated to "MKR" in this section. Her name appears as "Marjorie Kinnan Baskin" throughout the formal trial proceedings.

2. The trial archives (consisting of original court papers from the Alachua County Circuit Court, the three-volume trial transcript, trial depositions and exhibits, Florida Supreme Court records and briefs, legal correspondence, and the contents of Judge Murphree's and Philip May's files) are part of the Rawlings Collection, located in the Rare Books Room of the University of Florida Library in Gainesville, Florida. The Rawlings Collection also includes more than a thousand letters, from which the letters in this book were drawn. Some of these letters are reproduced in G. Bigelow and L. Monti, *Selected Letters of Marjorie Kinnan Rawlings* (University of Florida Press, 1983), and, where appropriate, citations to that work are included. With a few exceptions, the citations in this section refer only to directly quoted material in text. However, the trial records, correspondence, interviews, newspaper accounts, and other authorities cited herein are the source of all factual details contained in the book.

Letters of Marjorie Kinnan Rawlings (University of Florida Press, 1983), p. 266; hereafter, *"Selected Letters"*

7, 5   T.T., vol. III, p. 259 (testimony of MKR)

7, 32   *Cross Creek,* p. 9

8, 7   T.T., vol. III, p. 281 (testimony of MKR)

8, 20   Letter from MKR to Alfred S. Dashiell, March 1930, *Selected Letters,* p. 36

8, 36   T.T., vol. III, p. 261 (testimony of MKR)

10, 5   *Id.,* p. 264; letter from MKR to Alfred S. Dashiell, March 1930, *Selected Letters,* p. 36

11, 10 T.T., vol. III, p. 264 (testimony of MKR)

11, 17 Letter from MKR to Maxwell E. Perkins, Nov. 5, 1935, *Selected Letters,* p. 104

11, 20 Letter from MKR to Maxwell E. Perkins, Dec. 29, 1937, *Selected Letters,* p. 146

11, 24 Letter from MKR to Maxwell E. Perkins, June 8, 1938, *Selected Letters,* p. 156

11, 26 Letter from Maxwell E. Perkins to MKR, May 9, 1939

11, 29 T.T., vol. III, p. 265 (testimony of MKR)

11, 31 *Id.,* p. 346

12, 14 *Id.,* p. 264

12, 20 Declaration, *Cason v. Baskin,* Alachua County Circuit Court, no. 626-L (hereafter, "Trial Proceedings"), filed Feb. 1, 1943, pp. 2–3

12, 25 Pleas of Privilege, *id.,* filed March 3, 1945, p. 8

12, 28 T.T., vol. III, p. 346 (testimony of MKR)

12, 29 Letter from MKR to Maxwell E. Perkins, Sept. 15, 1941, *Selected Letters,* p. 209

13, 5   *Cross Creek,* p. 64

13, 11 T.T., vol. III, p. 326 (testimony of MKR)

13, 12 *Id.,* p. 312

13, 14 *Id.,* p. 296

13, 30 Letter from MKR to Editor, *Ocala Evening Star,* Jan. 31, 1931, *Selected Letters,* p. 39. Marjorie's lengthy letter was published in the Feb. 2, 1931, edition of the *Ocala Evening Star* (there dated Jan. 30, 1931).

14, 6   Letter from Max Perkins to MKR, April 10, 1931

14, 9   Letter from MKR to Philip S. May, Jan. 2, 1944

14, 14   M. Rawlings, "Cracker Chidlings" ("The Preacher Has His Fun") *Scribner's Magazine* 89 (Feb. 1931): 132

14, 31   T.T., vol. I, p. 81 (testimony of Zelma Cason)

15, 3   *Id.*, vol. III, p. 262 (testimony of MKR)

15, 11   *Id.*, p. 263; letter from MKR to Philip S. May, Jan. 2, 1944

15, 31   Letter from MKR to Maxwell E. Perkins, April 15, 1933, *Selected Letters*, p. 68

16, 6   Letter from MKR to Philip S. May, Feb. 5, 1943, *Selected Letters*, p. 234. Marjorie wrote about Ross Allen in the *Cross Creek* chapter "The Ancient Enmity," pp. 166–79.

16, 12   Letter from MKR to Maxwell E. Perkins, Aug. 27, 1936, *Selected Letters*, pp. 119–20

16, 22   Letter from Philip S. May to Lyon and Lyon, Esquires, Los Angeles, Dec. 28, 1943

16, 31   Letter from MKR to Maxwell E. Perkins, Sept. 15, 1941, *Selected Letters*, pp. 209–10

17, 9   Letter from Maxwell E. Perkins to MKR, Sept. 29, 1941

17, 22   Interview with J.T. Glisson, Evinston, Fla., March 25, 1986

18, 10   *Cross Creek*, p. 101

18, 15   T.T., vol. III, p. 269 (testimony of MKR)

18, 26   Letter from MKR to Philip S. May, Feb. 5, 1943, *Selected Letters*, p. 235

18, 31   Letter from MKR to Philip S. May, Nov. 26, 1945

20, 1   *Id.*

20, 8   *Id.*

20, 22   Letter from MKR to Philip S. May, May 1946

20, 23   Letter from A.N. (Annie) Slater to MKR, May 8, 1946

20, 29   Interview with Dessie Smith Prescott, Crystal River, Fla., March 25, 1986

20, 35   *Cross Creek*, p. 126

21, 11   Letter from Eva Fairbanks Glass to MKR, Nov. 4, 1942

21, 16 Letter from MKR to Eva Fairbanks Glass, Dec. 3, 1942

21, 27 Letter from MKR to Philip S. May, Feb. 5, 1943, *Selected Letters*, p. 232

21, 34 Letter from MKR to Philip S. May, Nov. 26, 1945

22, 12 N. Smiley, *Florida: Land of Images* (Miami: E. A. Seemann, 1972), p. 181; letter from MKR to Maxwell E. Perkins, June 5, 1946, *Selected Letters*, p. 287

22, 22 Letter from Ross Allen to MKR, Feb. 16, 1943

22, 29 Letter from MKR to Philip S. May, Nov. 26, 1945

22, 32 Letter from MKR to J. R. Tompkins, Sept. 21, 1945

23, 13 T.T., vol. III, p. 265 (testimony of MKR)

23, 20 *Id.*, p. 266

23, 30 *Id.*, p. 268

23, 32 Interview with J. T. Glisson, Evinston, Fla., Dec. 18, 1985

23, 36 Interview with Clare Hadley, Island Grove, Fla., March 28, 1986

24, 15 T.T., vol. I, p. 63 (testimony of Zelma Cason). Zelma believed that the meeting took place in March, rather than April, as Marjorie testified (*id.*, p. 64).

24, 20 *Id.*, vol. III, pp. 272–73 (testimony of MKR)

25, 6 Telephone interview with Idella Parker, Ocala, Fla., April 14, 1988. The unnamed reference to Idella as "the perfect maid" appears in *Cross Creek*, p. 203.

Chapter 2. My Friend Zelma

28, 9 T.T., vol. I, p. 42 (testimony of Zelma Cason)

28, 19 *Id.*, p. 64

29, 23 Answers to Interrogatories to Plaintiff, Trial Proceedings, filed Feb. 25, 1946, no. 59, p. 3

29, 28 T.T., vol. II, p. 254 (testimony of Carolyn McCollum)

29, 32 N. Smiley, *Florida: Land of Images*, (Miami: E. A. Seemann, 1972), p. 185

29, 37 Interview with J. T. Glisson, Evinston, Fla., Dec. 18, 1985

30, 5 Interview with Sigsbee Lee Scruggs, conducted and tape recorded by J. T. Glisson, Gainesville, Fla., 1978

30, 10   Interview with Clare Hadley, Island Grove, Fla., March 28, 1986

30, 19   Interview with Norton Baskin, St. Augustine, Fla., Dec. 17, 1985

31, 1   Interview with Clare Hadley, Island Grove, Fla., March 28, 1986

31, 8   T.T., vol. I, p. 65 (testimony of Zelma Cason)

31, 19   Declaration, Trial Proceedings, filed Feb. 1, 1943, p. 1

31, 29   T.T., vol. I, p. 148 (testimony of Noel Moore)

31, 31   *Id.*, vol, II, p. 225 (testimony of Mrs. Freddie Lee Whitlock)

31, 33   *Id.*, p. 233 (testimony of Willard Howatt)

32, 9   *Id.*, p. 239 (testimony of Dessie Smith)

32, 26   *Id.*, vol. I, p. 48 (testimony of Zelma Cason); vol. III, p. 287 (testimony of MKR)

32, 27   Deposition of Mrs. A.N. Slater, Warrenville, S.C., May 15, 1946, p. 4 (Defendants' Exhibit no. 13, Trial Proceedings)

32, 34   T.T., vol. I, p. 59 (testimony of Zelma Cason)

33, 10   Letter from MKR to Philip S. May, Jan. 8, 1948

33, 31   Letter from MKR to Philip S. May, Jan. 12, 1944, *Selected Letters*, p. 245

34, 2   *Id.*

34, 15   T.T., vol. I, p. 70 (testimony of Zelma Cason)

34, 22   *Id.*, vol. III, pp. 261, 290 (testimony of MKR)

34, 35   Letter from MKR to Philip S. May, Dec. 19, 1945

35, 2   Letter from MKR to Philip S. May, Feb. 27, 1945, *Selected Letters*, p. 259

35, 8   T.T., vol. III, p. 270 (testimony of MKR)

35, 15   *Id.*

Chapter 3. A Declaration of War

36, 29   Trumbull, "Rawlings Trial—Noteworthy Book Come to Life," *Miami Herald*, May 26, 1946, p. 1

37, 26   Interview with William Townsend, Palatka, Fla., March 27, 1986

38, 5   Interview with Parks Carmichael, Gainesville, Fla., Dec. 11, 1985
38, 9   Telephone interview with Mrs. Lois W. Townsend, Palatka, Fla., July 2, 1987
38, 14 Letter from MKR to Philip S. May, Nov. 11, 1946. The report came from a young (unidentified) writer who had vacationed near the Walton cottage the previous year.
38, 19 "Private Services Set for 'Miss Kate,'" *Palatka Daily News*, Jan. 8, 1985, p. 1
38, 27 Interview with Stephen L. Boyles, Palatka, Fla., March 27, 1986
40, 14 T.T., vol. I, p. 49 (testimony of Zelma Cason)
40, 23 *Id.*, p. 55
40, 28 *Id.*, p. 61
40, 35 Letter from MKR to Philip S. May, Feb. 27, 1945, *Selected Letters*, p. 259
41, 8   T.T., vol. II, p. 237 (testimony of Mae DuPree)
41, 15 Deposition of Mrs. Ida M. Tarrant, St. Augustine, Fla., March 30, 1945, p. 14 (Defendants' Exhibit no. 14, Trial Proceedings)
41, 17 T.T., vol. I, p. 56 (testimony of Zelma Cason)
41, 26 Letter from MKR to Philip S. May, Jan. 13, 1943
41, 28 Letter from MKR to Philip S. May, Feb. 5, 1943, *Selected Letters*, p. 235
41, 32 Letter from MKR to Philip S. May, April 10, 1943
41, 35 Letter from MKR to Philip S. May, May 1, 1943
42, 1   Letter from MKR to Philip S. May, Oct. 24, 1943
42, 5   Letter from MKR to Philip S. May, Dec. 31, 1945 (reproduced in part), *Selected Letters*, p. 277
42, 20 Letter from Ross Allen to MKR, Feb. 16, 1943
43, 12 Letter from "Bob" (Robert Camp?) to Philip S. May, July 7, 1947. The supervisor was identified as Kenneth Van Der Hulse (*id.*).
43, 24 T.T., vol. I, p. 136 (testimony of Mrs. J. Edward Preston)
43, 33 *Id.*, p. 104 (testimony of Zelma Cason)
44, 3   *Id.*, vol. III, p. 340 (testimony of Dr. T. Z. Cason)
44, 21 *Id.*, vol. II, p. 237 (testimony of Mae DuPree); *id.*, vol.

III, p. 369 (testimony of Zelma Cason)

44, 33   Interview with Sigsbee Lee Scruggs, conducted and tape-recorded by J. T. Glisson, Gainesville, Fla., 1978

45, 8   Interview with Norton Baskin, St. Augustine, Fla., Dec. 17, 1985

45, 23   Letter from MKR to Philip S. May, Jan. 2, 1944

45, 28   Interview with Clare Hadley, Island Grove, Fla., March 28, 1986

46, 12   Interview with William Townsend, Palatka, Fla., March 27, 1986

47, 3   T.T., vol. I, p. 91 (testimony of Zelma Cason); *id.*, vol. III, p. 343 (testimony of Dr. T. Z. Cason)

48, 1   Letter from MKR to Philip S. May, Nov. 11, 1946. Marjorie did not reveal the name of the young writer.

48, 5   Telephone interview with Lois W. Townsend, Palatka, Fla., July 2, 1987

48, 15   J. Carson, *Florida Common Law Pleading Practice and Procedure* (Atlanta: The Harrison Co., 1949), p. 78

48, 21   *Cason v. Baskin,* 159 Fla. 31, 34, 30 So.2d 635, 637 (1947) (Second Appeal)

48, 29   Chap. 21932, Laws of 1943, F.S.A. Sec. 708.08–.10. Among other provisions, the act provided that a married woman could "sue and be sued" without the joinder of her husband, *id.* Sec. 708.08. The Florida Supreme Court in response to Marjorie's first appeal declared that the joinder of Marjorie's husband, Norton Baskin, as a party defendant was a "formality later rendered unnecessary" by the adoption of the act; see *Cason v. Baskin,* 155 Fla. 198, 200, 20 So.2d 243, 244 (Fla. 1944) (First Appeal).

49, 2   Declaration, Trial Proceedings, filed Feb. 1, 1943, p. 1, 2, 6, 8, 10, 11. In her declaration, Zelma complained of several references to herself in *Cross Creek.* See *Cross Creek,* pp. 48–49, 52, 53, 54–55, 147, 285.

50, 13   T.T., vol. III, p. 363 (testimony of MKR)

50, 21   Letter from MKR to Philip S. May, Feb. 5, 1943, *Selected Letters,* p. 230

Chapter 4. Warfare by Pleading

51, 4   Interview with J. T. Glisson, Evinston, Fla., Dec. 18, 1985

51, 16   T.T., vol. III, pp. 333–34 (testimony of MKR)

52, 20   Trumbull, "Rawlings Trial—Noteworthy Book Come to Life," *Miami Herald*, May 26, 1946, p. 1

54, 6   Letter from MKR to Philip S. May, Feb. 5, 1943, *Selected Letters*, p. 231

54, 21   Letter from MKR to Philip S. May, Jan. 13, 1943

54, 24   Letter from MKR to Philip S. May, Feb. 5, 1943, *Selected Letters*, p. 231

54, 31   Letter from Philip S. May to MKR, Jan. 19, 1943. The passage that caused May concern was a paragraph that began: "My profane friend Zelma, the census taker, said . . ." and went on to quote edited snatches of profanity (*id.;* see *Cross Creek*, p. 147).

55, 1   Demurrer to Declaration, Trial Proceedings, filed Feb. 26, 1943, p. 1

55, 10   Letter from "Crawford and May" to the Hon. John A. H. Murphree, April 7, 1943

55, 13   Letter from MKR to Philip S. May, April 10, 1943

55, 26   Letter from Philip S. May to MKR, July 1, 1943

56, 4   Letter from Philip S. May to MKR, Aug. 9, 1943

56, 16   Letter from Philip S. May to MKR, Oct. 20, 1943

56, 24   Letter from MKR to Philip S. May, Oct. 24, 1943

56, 30   Letter from Philip S. May to MKR, Oct. 30, 1943

56, 34   Letter from MKR to Philip S. May, Jan. 2, 1944

57, 8   Letter from Philip S. May to MKR, Dec. 31, 1943

57, 22   Initial Brief of Appellant, *Cason v. Baskin*, Florida Supreme Court (First Appeal), filed Dec. 27, 1943, pp. 4–5, 30, 33

58, 1   *Id.*, p. 32

58, 8   Letter from MKR to Philip S. May, Jan. 2, 1944

58, 23   Letter from Philip S. May to MKR, Feb. 10, 1944

58, 28   Letter from MKR to Philip S. May, Feb. 5, 1944

59, 9   *Cason v. Baskin*, 155 Fla. 198, 212, 20 So.2d 243, 250 (1944) (First Appeal)

59, 14   *Id.*, at 205–7, 20 So.2d 246–47

59, 34   *Id.*, at 220, 20 So.2d at 253. The dissenting opinion, in which two justices joined, did not dispute the majority's recognition of the right of privacy. Instead, it urged that Zelma's privacy had not been invaded, because the book had only portrayed her conduct "while performing the functions of a public servant in the office of census enumerator." See *id.*, at 222, 20 So.2d at 254 (Buford, C. J., dissenting).

60, 4   Letter from Philip S. May to MKR, Nov. 25, 1944

60, 12   Letter from MKR to Philip S. May (undated, but probably written Nov. 25, 1944)

60, 25   Letter from MKR to Philip S. May, Nov. 27, 1944

Chapter 5. On to Courtroom Battle

64, 25   Interview with Sigsbee Lee Scruggs, conducted and tape-recorded by J.T. Glisson, Gainesville, Fla., 1978

65, 18   Interview with Sigsbee Lee Scruggs, Jr., Gainesville, Fla., Aug. 15, 1986

66, 13   *Id.*

66, 24   Interview with Clara Floyd Gehan, Gainesville, Fla., Aug. 14, 1986

67, 2   Interview with Parks Carmichael, Gainesville, Fla., Dec. 11, 1985

67, 7   Interview with Sigsbee Lee Scruggs, Jr., Gainesville, Fla., Aug. 15, 1986

67, 24   The story of Samson and Henry is related in the chapter "Black Shadows," *Cross Creek*, pp. 193–201. Sigsbee Scruggs is the unnamed lawyer (*id.* at 200–201).

68, 4   Letter from MKR to Philip S. May, Jan. 26, 1945

68, 11   Letter from Sigsbee Lee Scruggs to Philip S. May, Feb. 10, 1945

68, 23   Letter from Philip S. May to MKR, Feb. 12, 1945

69, 6   Pleas, Trial Proceedings, filed March 3, 1945, pp. 1–2, 8–9

69, 24   Letter from Philip S. May to MKR, June 15, 1945

70, 5   Letter from MKR to Philip S. May, Nov. 8, 1945
70, 31 Letter from MKR to Philip S. May, Dec. 31, 1945 (reproduced in part), *Selected Letters*, pp. 276–77
71, 22 Letter from Philip S. May to MKR, Nov. 29, 1945
71, 35 Quotation contained in letter from MKR to Philip S. May, Jan. 13, 1943
72, 3   Letter from Philip S. May to MKR, April 22, 1943
72, 9   Letter from Philip S. May to Charles Scribner, Aug. 18, 1943
72, 33 Letter from Edward N. Perkins to Philip S. May, Jan. 16, 1946
73, 3   Letter from MKR to Philip S. May, March 21, 1946, *Selected Letters*, p. 279
73, 21 Letter from MKR to Philip S. May, April 12, 1946. Edward Perkins had, in fact, reduced his fee from $300 to $250 plus expenses, at May's suggestion (letter from Edward N. Perkins to Philip S. May, March 15, 1946; letter from Philip S. May to Edward N. Perkins, March 19, 1946).
74, 1   Letter from Philip S. May to MKR, Nov. 13, 1945
74, 11 A well-known biographer estimated the legal fees at "more than $18,000" (G. Bigelow, *Frontier Eden: The Literary Career of Marjorie Kinnan Rawlings* [Gainesville: University of Florida Press, 1966], p. 44). Norton Baskin believes that the figure was at least that high (interview with Norton Baskin, St. Augustine, Fla., July 2, 1987).
74, 21 Letter from MKR to Philip S. May, Jan. 13, 1943
74, 26 Letter from MKR to Philip S. May, Oct. 24, 1943
74, 34 Letter from Philip S. May to MKR, Jan. 4, 1944
75, 6   Letter from MKR to Philip S. May, Jan. 5, 1944
75, 22 Letter from MKR to Philip S. May, Dec. 4, 1944
75, 31 Letter from MKR to Philip S. May, April 18, 1946, *Selected Letters*, p. 283
76, 12 Letter from MKR to Philip S. May, June 15, 1945
76, 17 Letter from MKR to Philip S. May, March 21, 1946, *Selected Letters*, p. 279
76, 31 Interview with Clare Hadley, Island Grove, Fla., March 28, 1986

77, 1   Letter from MKR to Philip S. May, April 18, 1946,
          Selected Letters, p. 281
77, 13   *Id., Selected Letters*, pp. 282–83
78, 6   Letter from MKR to Philip S. May, April 12, 1946

Chapter 6. *The* Cross Creek *Trial*

79, 17   Letter from Philip S. May to the Hon. Gordon B.
          Knowles, May 30, 1946
79, 19   Keen, "The Book That Shook Cross Creek," *Gaines-
          ville Sun*, Oct. 10, 1982, p. 9A
79, 20   Letter from MKR to Maxwell E. Perkins, June 5,
          1946, *Selected Letters*, p. 286; letter from MKR to
          Philip S. May, June 1, 1946
79, 21   Interview with Ioleen Cody, Gainesville, Fla., Nov.
          25, 1985
80, 1   Trumbull, "Cross Creek Court Drama Begins
          Today," *Miami Herald*, May 20, 1946, p. 1
80, 21   Proby, "A Case of Privacy," *Miami Herald, Tropic
          Magazine*, Dec. 13, 1981, p. 44. Ms. Proby, then a
          University of Florida student, attended the entire
          trial.
81, 6   "Miss Cason Testifies In Trial of Author," *Gainesville
          Daily Sun*, May 21, 1946, p. 6; interview with Norton
          Baskin, St. Augustine Fla., Dec. 17, 1985
81, 19   Clendinen, "Witness Says 'Cross Creek' Is Litera-
          ture," *Tampa Morning Tribune*, May 23, 1946, p. 12
83, 19   Trumbull, "Rawlings Trial—Noteworthy Book
          Come to Life," *Miami Herald*, May 26, 1946, p. 2A
83, 33   Interview with John Murphree, Jr., Gainesville, Fla.,
          Aug. 13, 1986
84, 1   Letter from MKR to Philip S. May, Feb. 5, 1943,
          Selected Letters, p. 231
84, 10   Fla. Stat. Sec. 40.01 (1949)
84, 29   T.T., vol. I, p. 20
84, 32   "Miss Cason Testifies In Trial Of Author," *Gaines-
          ville Daily Sun*, May 21, 1946, p. 6
85, 7   Letter from Philip S. May to MKR, March 19, 1946

86, 1   Interview with Norton Baskin, St. Augustine, Fla., March 24, 1986

86, 33   T.T., vol. I, pp. 67–69, 73 (testimony of Zelma Cason)

87, 34   *Id.*, p. 96

88, 7   *Id.*, p. 95

89, 30   *Id.*, p. 106

89, 36   *Id.*, pp. 116–17

90, 11   *Id.*, p. 120 (testimony of Bert Ergle)

90, 16   *Id.*, p. 123

90, 27   *Id.*, pp. 123–24 (testimony of Mary Carn)

91, 3   *Id.*, p. 125

91, 23   *Id.*, pp. 129, 132 (testimony of Alice M. Ellis)

92, 5   *Id.*, p. 136 (testimony of Mrs. J. Edward Preston)

92, 19   *Id.*, pp. 148–49 (testimony of Noel Moore)

93, 3   *Id.*, p. 151

93, 21   *Id.*, pp. 156–57 (testimony of Mrs. Chase Maddox, Jr.)

93, 28   *Id.*, vol. II, pp. 254–55 (testimony of Mrs. J. W. McCollum)

94, 4   *Id.*, p. 246 (testimony of Tom Glisson)

94, 9   *Id.*, pp. 166, 168 (testimony of Thelma Shortridge)

94, 20   *Id.*, pp. 224–25 (testimony of Freddie Lee Whitlock)

94, 31   *Id.*, p. 241 (testimony of Carey Dyess)

94, 35   *Id.*, p. 236 (testimony of Verle Pope)

95, 19   *Id.*, p. 246

96, 1   *Id.*, p. 170 (testimony of Dr. Alfred J. Hanna)

96, 8   *Id.*, pp. 178, 172

96, 21   *Id.*, pp. 196, 200 (testimony of Dr. Clifford P. Lyons)

97, 8   Interview with Norton Baskin, St. Augustine, Fla., Dec. 17, 1985

97, 25   T.T., vol. II, p. 191, 194 (testimony of Lt. Bertram C. Cooper)

98, 14   Deposition of James R. Peters, Lansing, Michigan, April 12, 1946, p. 6 (Defendants' Exhibit no. 9, Trial Proceedings)

98, 29   T.T., vol. II, p. 178 (testimony of Dr. Alfred J. Hanna)

98, 36   *Cross Creek*, p. 22

99, 2   T.T., vol. II, pp. 179–80 (testimony of Dr. Alfred J. Hanna)

99, 20 *Cross Creek,* pp. 11–12

99, 21 T.T., vol. II, pp. 181–82 (testimony of Dr. Alfred J. Hanna)

100, 12 *Cross Creek,* pp. 106–7

100, 13 T.T., vol. II, p. 219 (testimony of Dr. Clifford P. Lyons)

100, 17 *Cross Creek,* pp. 57–58

100, 20 T.T., vol. II, pp. 221, 223 (testimony of Dr. Clifford P. Lyons)

100, 34 Trumbull, "Saturdays Are Sacred So Author Must Wait," *Miami Herald,* May 25, 1946, p. 1

Chapter 7. *The Jury Returns*

102, 13 Interview with Norton Baskin, St. Augustine, Fla., Dec. 17, 1985

102, 15 Clendinen, "Mrs. Rawlings Defends Her 'Cross Creek,'" *Tampa Morning Tribune,* May 25, 1946, p. 1

102, 29 T.T., vol. III, p. 257 (testimony of MKR)

103, 10 *Id.,* p. 261

103, 14 Anderson, "Mrs. Rawlings Says She Was Charmed By Floridians," *Gainesville Daily Sun,* May 24, 1946, p. 1

103, 16 T.T., vol. III, p. 264 (testimony of MKR)

103, 35 *Id.,* p. 266

104, 3 *Id.,* pp. 267–68

105, 3 *Id.,* p. 270

105, 19 *Id.,* p. 279

106, 4 *Id.,* pp. 281–82

106, 21 *Cross Creek,* p. 205

106, 25 T.T., vol. III, p. 283 (testimony of MKR)

106, 34 *Id.,* p. 297

107, 2 *Id.,* pp. 297, 299–300

107, 13 *Id.,* pp. 302–4

108, 1 *Cross Creek,* pp. 185–89

108, 8 T.T., vol. III, p. 309 (testimony of MKR)

108, 15 Trumbull, "Saturdays Are Sacred So Author Must Wait," *Miami Herald*, May 25, 1946, p. 2A

108, 21 "Author Denies Cruel Intent Toward 'Cross Creek' Folk," (Jacksonville) *Florida Times-Union*, May 28, 1946, p. 1

108, 22 T.T., vol. III, pp. 312, 314 (testimony of MKR)

109, 6 *Id.*, pp. 318, 327–28

109, 17 *Id.*, p. 321

109, 28 Letter from Eva Fairbanks Glass to MKR, Nov. 4, 1942

109, 30 *Cross Creek*, pp. 108–21

109, 36 T.T., vol. III, p. 322 (testimony of MKR). After lengthy arguments outside the hearing of the jury, portions of Mrs. Glass's letter and Marjorie's reply were offered into evidence (*id.*, pp. 365–69; Plaintiff's Exhibits nos. 4 and 5, Trial Proceedings)

110, 6 T.T., vol. III, p. 335 (testimony of MKR)

110, 36 *Id.*, p. 344

111, 5 *Id.*

111, 19 *Id.*, p. 346

113, 9 Trumbull, "Jury May Get Rawlings Suit Late Today," *Miami Herald*, May 28, 1946, p. 4A

113, 24 *Id.*

113, 31 Letter from MKR to Maxwell E. Perkins, June 5, 1946, *Selected Letters*, p. 286

114, 4 T.T., vol. III, pp. 363–64 (testimony of MKR)

114, 16 *Id.*, pp. 369–70 (testimony of Zelma Cason)

115, 2 Anderson, "Attorneys Argue Rawlings Case As Testimony Is Ended," *Gainesville Daily Sun*, May 28, 1946, p. 1

115, 10 Trumbull, "Author of 'Cross Creek' Wins Her Privacy Suit," *Miami Herald*, May 29, 1946, p. 4A; Anderson, "Attorneys Argue Rawlings Case As Testimony Is Ended," *Gainesville Daily Sun*, May 28, 1946, p. 1; Proby, "A Case of Privacy," *Miami Herald, Tropic Magazine*, Dec. 13, 1981, p. 43

115, 37 Trumbull, "Author of 'Cross Creek' Wins Her Privacy Suit," *Miami Herald*, May 29, 1946, p. 4A

116, 5 *Id.*; interview with Sigsbee Lee Scruggs, conducted and tape-recorded by J. T. Glisson, Gainesville, Fla., 1978

117, 2 Trumbull, "Author of 'Cross Creek' Wins Her Privacy Suit," *Miami Herald*, May 29, 1946, p. 4A

117, 33 *Id.*, p. 1

118, 11 Letter from MKR to Maxwell E. Perkins, June 5, 1946, *Selected Letters*, p. 287

Chapter 8. A Hollow Victory

119, 10 Letter from Philip S. May to MKR, May 29, 1946

119, 15 Letter from MKR to Philip S. May, June 1, 1946

119, 19 Letter from Philip S. May to MKR, June 5, 1946

120, 9 Letter from Stella Thacker to MKR, May 30, 1946

120, 28 Letter from Whitney Darrow to Philip S. May, June 5, 1946

121, 9 "Marjorie Kinnan Rawlings Wins Important Case in Florida Courts," *Publishers Weekly*, June 29, 1946, pp. 3328–29

121, 21 Letter from MKR to the Editors, *Time*, June 14, 1946

122, 6 Letter from Whitney Darrow to Philip S. May, June 11, 1946

122, 15 Letter from Philip S. May to J. T. G. Crawford, July 16, 1946

123, 2 Letter from Philip S. May to MKR, July 18, 1946

123, 6 Letter from MKR to Sigsbee Lee Scruggs, July 25, 1946, *Selected Letters*, p. 288 (there dated July 23, 1946)

123, 19 Letter from Philip S. May to MKR, July 26, 1946

123, 27 Letter from A. J. Cronin to MKR, July 27, 1946

124, 7 Letter from Philip S. May to MKR, June 11, 1946

124, 13 Letter from MKR to Philip S. May, Aug. 28, 1946

124, 19 Letter from Maxwell E. Perkins to MKR, June 20, 1946

124, 24 Letter from MKR to Maxwell E. Perkins, June 5, 1946, *Selected Letters*, p. 287

124, 29 Letter from MKR to Sigrid Arne, June 15, 1946

125, 14 Letter from MKR to Maxwell E. Perkins, April 11, 1945, *Selected Letters*, p. 263

125, 18 Letter from MKR to Ellen Glasgow, Nov. 9, 1945, *Selected Letters*, p. 275

125, 23 Letter from MKR to Maxwell E. Perkins, Feb. 13, 1947

125, 25 Letter from MKR to Bee McNeil, Jan. 26, 1952

125, 32 Letter from James Branch Cabell to MKR, June 1, 1946

126, 5 Letter from James Branch Cabell to MKR, Sept. 4, 1949

126, 12 Letter from MKR to Ellen Glasgow, May 24, 1944, *Selected Letters*, p. 251

126, 20 Letter from MKR to Ellen Glasgow, Oct. 7, 1943

126, 22 Letter from MKR to "Aunt" Ida Tarrant, Jan. 11, 1944

126, 24 Letter from MKR to Maxwell E. Perkins, May 3, 1944, *Selected Letters*, p. 249

127, 6 Letter from MKR to Bee McNeil, Dec. 14, 1950

127, 22 Letter from MKR to Carl Van Vechten, July 8, 1948, *Selected Letters*, p. 315

128, 1 Letter from MKR to Bernice Gilkyson, July 9, 1947, *Selected Letters*, p. 300

128, 21 Letter from MKR to John Hall Wheelock, June 12, 1952, *Selected Letters*, pp. 373–74

128, 31 Letter from MKR to Norman Berg, Feb. 4, 1949, *Selected Letters*, p. 322

129, 3 Letter from Philip S. May to MKR, July 23, 1948

129, 16 Letter from MKR to Norman Berg, April 13, 1950, *Selected Letters*, p. 352

129, 19 Letter from MKR to Philip S. May, Nov. 24, 1948, *Selected Letters*, p. 320; see also letter from MKR to Philip S. May, June 26, 1947

129, 27 Letter from Philip S. May to MKR, Dec. 9, 1948

130, 1 Letter from MKR to Norman Berg, Feb. 21, 1947, *Selected Letters*, p. 291

Chapter 9. The Battle Won, the War Lost

131, 24 Memorandum from J. T. G. Crawford to Philip S. May, Feb. 19, 1947

132, 8   Letter from Philip S. May to Guyte P. McCord, clerk of the Florida Supreme Court, April 12, 1947

132, 23   *Cason v. Baskin*, 159 Fla. 31, 37, 40, 30 So.2d 635, 638, 640 (1947) (Second Appeal)

134, 13   *Id.* at 41, 30 So.2d at 640. The decision was four to three, the justice absent from the oral argument having joined in the decision. A dissenting opinion, in which two of the three dissenters joined, urged that the trial court had erred in overruling Zelma's demurrer to two of the defendants' amended pleas, and that the judgment should be reversed and a new trial ordered. See *id.* at 41, 52, 30 So.2d at 641, 646 (Chapman, J., dissenting).

134, 24   Letter from Philip S. May to MKR, May 23, 1947

134, 28   Letter from Maxwell E. Perkins to MKR, May 29, 1947

135, 4   Letter from Philip S. May to the Hon. John A. H. Murphree, Feb. 2, 1949

135, 28   Letter from MKR to Philip S. May, June 26, 1947

136, 14   Motion for Clarification of Opinion and Mandate, *Cason v. Baskin*, Florida Supreme Court (Second Appeal) filed Jan. 2, 1948, p. 2

136, 26   Letter from MKR to Philip S. May, Jan. 8, 1948

137, 11   Letter from MKR to Philip S. May, March 30, 1948, *Selected Letters*, p. 312

137, 16   *Id.*

137, 18   Letter from MKR to Philip S. May, April 12, 1948

137, 27   Letter from MKR to Philip S. May, Sept. 30, 1947

137, 35   Letter from Philip S. May to MKR, Oct. 7, 1947

138, 4   Letter from MKR to Philip S. May, June 26, 1947. The proposed letter to the justices of the Florida Supreme Court was contained in the letter to May. There is no evidence that it was ever sent, and there was apparently no reply from the court. But cf. *Selected Letters*, p. 317.

139, 7   Letter from Walton and Walton to the Hon. John A. H. Murphree, July 19, 1948

139, 24   Letter from MKR to Philip S. May, Aug. 10, 1948, *Selected Letters*, pp. 316–17

141, 27   Letter from Walton and Walton to Philip S. May, Aug. 9, 1948

141, 30   Letter from Philip S. May to Whitney Darrow, Aug. 11, 1948

142, 3   Letter from MKR to Philip S. May, Aug. 13, 1948

142, 23   Letter from MKR to Philip S. May, Nov. 24, 1948, *Selected Letters*, p. 320

Epilogue. Friends

144, 20   Interview with Norton Baskin, St. Augustine, Fla., Dec. 17, 1985; Keen, "The Book That Shook Cross Creek," *Gainesville Sun,* Oct. 10, 1982, p. 9A

145, 5   *Id.*

146, 8   A. Burt, "Al Burt's Florida: Cross Creek Reaches a Crossroad," *Miami Herald, Tropic Magazine,* March 11, 1984, p. 22

146, 20   *Cross Creek,* p. 368

147, 1   Letter from Snow and Ella Mae Slater to Norton Baskin, Jan. 8, 1954

Sources and Acknowledgments

No one can visit Marjorie Kinnan Rawlings's old farmhouse at Cross Creek without feeling a jumble of emotions. Here she started a new life in an exotically remote part of the world; here she fought the frost and mended the fences and fed the chickens; here she found the inspiration to stay on, alone; here she wrote and became a world-renowned author; here was her heart's true home, until the day she died.

I felt all of this when I first visited Marjorie's home at Cross Creek in October of 1985. I was a Yankee myself, on leave from the faculty of the University of Iowa College of Law, transplanted temporarily to the University of Florida in Gainesville, about eighteen miles from Cross Creek. Until then I had known Marjorie only through her writings. I visited Cross Creek again and again, and I came to know something of the warmth of the people and the natural beauty of rural northern Florida. I could understand the instincts that led Marjorie to this place and gave her the courage to press on in her work.

As a lawyer and law professor, I was interested to learn about a still-famous trial that had taken place in Gainesville in the 1940s. I was told that the trial records were housed in the Rare Books Room at the University of Florida Library, along with original manuscripts of Marjorie's writings and voluminous correspondence between Marjorie and her friends, family, editors, and attorneys. I decided to investigate, and the more I read, the more interested I became. But the lawsuit was difficult to decipher, with its prolix pleadings and procedural intricacies. I decided that with my background in law, I might help to construct a readable account of this complex case.

I am grateful to the many people who helped in this effort, beginning with Carmen Hurff and Sidney Ives of the University of Florida Rare Books Room, where the trial records are housed, and Theron A. Yawn III, an assistant state attorney who gathered and assembled the records. I also wish to acknowledge the support of the National Endowment for the Humanities through its Travel-to-Collections Grant.

Over forty years after the Cross Creek trial, there are many people still living and working in northern Florida who knew Marjorie and Zelma or participated in some phase of the trial. My interviews with them were an essential part of this book, and I thank them all for their kindness. Norton Baskin, Marjorie's husband, generously gave his time, sharing interesting and humorous recollections about the trial. I wish to especially thank him for permission to use the poem that is the epigraph of this book, written by Marjorie in her own hand on a sheet of yellow legal paper during the trial. The poem was found by Philip May, Jr., in 1987, folded in half and stuck between the pages of one of Marjorie's old school cookbooks. J.T. ("Jake") Glisson and his wife, Pat, opened their home to me and introduced me to many of the people mentioned in *Cross Creek*. Jake and his parents were already living at the Creek when Marjorie arrived in 1928, and his memories of people and events have been priceless. Jake did the splendid illustrations for this book, shared with me the "bridge" story, and allowed me to use his tape-recorded interview with Sigsbee Scruggs. Clare Hadley of Winter Park, the daughter of Dr. T.Z. Cason, met with me in the Cason house in Island Grove. I am indebted to her for her candid and affectionate memories of her aunt, Zelma Cason.

Several people were most helpful and generous in providing information about the attorneys involved in Zelma's lawsuit. E. A. Clayton, the Waltons's co-counsel, and Parks Carmichael, Sigsbee Scruggs's law partner, spoke to me in Gainesville about their involvement in the case. Philip May, Jr., of Jacksonville shared his recollections about the work of his father, Marjorie's friend and attorney, Philip May. Sigsbee Lee Scruggs, Jr., of Gainesville told me delightful stories about his father, who co-counseled the case with May; I also enjoyed a visit with Mrs. Sigsbee Scruggs in the Scruggs home. William Townsend of Palatka, an attorney with the Walton firm, talked to me about his aunt, Kate Walton, and his grandfather, J. V. Walton. I appreciate the information shared by Lois W. Townsend, Kate Walton's sister, Stephen Lewis Boyles, who practiced with the Walton firm late in Kate's career, and George Newton, a former stenographer with the Walton firm. I thank attorney Clara Floyd Gehan of Gainesville for her reminiscences about Kate Walton and Sigsbee Scruggs, and John Murphree, Jr., of Gainesville for his recollections of his father, Judge John A. H. Murphree.

Many other people gave freely of their time: Dessie Smith Prescott of Crystal River, about whom Marjorie wrote in "Hyacinth Drift"; Idella Parker, who was Marjorie's maid and friend for many years; Harry Evans, postmaster of Island Grove; Mrs. Chet Crosby of Island Grove and Mrs Raymond Boyt of Citra, who talked to me about Zelma and Marjorie; Ioleen Cody of Gainesville, who attended the trial; and Hampton Dunn of Tampa, whose coverage of the trial for the *Tampa Daily Times* won an Associated Dailies of Florida award. Thanks, too, to Dr. Samuel Proctor of the Florida State Museum, Dr. Michael Gannon of the University of

Florida College of Liberal Arts, and Sally Morrison, who was caretaker of the Marjorie Kinnan Rawlings home at Cross Creek. I also appreciate the excellent editorial assistance of the staff of University Presses of Florida, the work of my secretary, Fran Swanson, and the help of the Hon. Richard Acton in compiling the index of this book.

I wish to give special thanks to Dr. Gordon Bigelow, author of *Frontier Eden: The Literary Career of Marjorie Kinnan Rawlings* (University of Florida Press, 1966) and co-editor of *Selected Letters of Marjorie Kinnan Rawlings* (University of Florida Press, 1983), for his encouragement of this work and for his valuable contributions to the literature about Marjorie Kinnan Rawlings. And I wish to acknowledge the contribution of Elizabeth Silverthorne to this body of literature by the publication of her recent biography, *Marjorie Kinnan Rawlings, Sojourner at Cross Creek* (Overlook Press, 1988). I also acknowledge the assistance of the University of Florida College of Law Library, the Ocala Public Library, and the court administrator of the Alachua County Circuit Court.

The story of the lawsuit and its aftermath is perceived here through the lens of its personalities and players. But those closest to the case knew that it transcended the consequences to their own lives and interests. Marjorie and Phil May were always concerned about the impact of the lawsuit on an author's freedom to write. They judged correctly that the case would leave its mark. It was among those in the forefront of the movement to recognize an individual's privacy as a protectable legal right. The Florida Supreme Court's decision in the first appeal represented the first recognition of the so-called "right of privacy" in Florida. At the time, only about one-fourth of the states had acknowledged the right in some form. *Cason v. Baskin* was therefore a leading case in the developing law of privacy, and it has been widely cited as precedent for such privacy issues as the existence of the right itself, the measure of damages, available defenses, and the strains between individual interests in privacy and public interest in free speech.

The decision has not, however, spawned the body of case law that Marjorie and Phil May feared it would. As May repeatedly emphasized, this lawsuit was apparently the first attempt by a literary subject to sue the author of an autobiographical work for invasion of privacy. May believed that the court's ruling would severely restrict an author's ability to write freely about factual subjects, and that *Cason v. Baskin* would be frequently cited in later cases for such a restrictive purpose. This has not occurred. When the case is cited as authority, it is for general privacy law issues; the specific factual context has played little role in subsequent decisions. Biographies and autobiographies abound in today's bookstores. Perhaps authors have learned the hard lesson Marjorie learned: when in doubt, obtain a subject's consent, or at least avoid stingingly humorous portrayals. More likely, the private interest/public interest issue addressed in *Cason v. Baskin* has resulted in a more favorable balance for the author today than it did in that case, where the public's interest in Zelma was held not to outweigh her right of privacy. As one authority summarized it: "It would be a strange rule which, in the case of a biographical work concerning a public figure, would penalize the naming, if somewhat embarrassing, of all persons who are not themselves public figures; and not surprisingly *Cason v. Baskin* seems to be unique" (Hill, *Defamation and Privacy Under the First Amendment,* 76 COLUM. L. REV. 1205, 1257 n. 243 [1976]).

Cason v. Baskin is indeed unique today, but for reasons that perhaps even Marjorie and May might relish, rather than regret, if they could only know.

Index

Library of Congress Cataloging-in-Publication Data

Acton, Patricia Nassif.
    Invasion of privacy : the Cross Creek trial of
Marjorie Kinnan Rawlings / Patricia Nassif Acton.
        p.   cm.
    Includes index.
    ISBN 0-8130-0906-5 (alk. paper)
    1. Cason, Zelma. 1890–1963—Trials, litigation, etc. 2. Rawlings,
Marjorie Kinnan, 1896–1953—Trials, litigation, etc. 3. Privacy,
Right of—Florida. 4. Rawlings, Marjorie Kinnan. 1896–1953. Cross
Creek. 5. Authors, American—20th century—Biography. 6. Cross
Creek (Fla.)—Biography. I. Title.
KF228.C34A27   1986
342.73'0858—dc19
    [347.302858]   88-12036
                                                                CIP